Dragoj Branku za sjećanje na jedan
bratski susret u Dubrovniku.

Božidar

Dubrovnik, 1. 8. 1973. godine

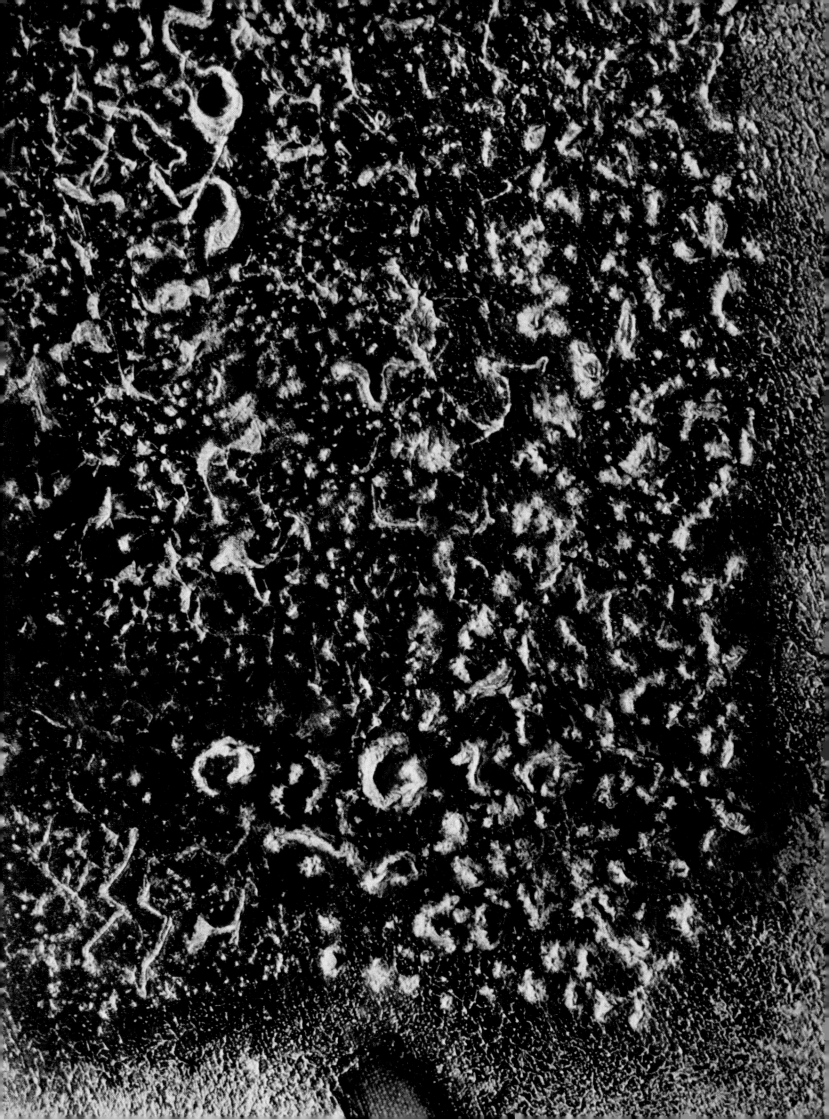

YUGOSLAVIA — LAND AND PEOPLE

YUGOSLAVIA (the Socialist Federative Republic of Yugoslavia) consists of six socialist republics: Slovenia, Croatia, Bosnia and Herzegovina, Serbia, Crna Gora (Montenegro), and Macedonia. The autonomous provinces of Vojvodina, Kosovo and Metohija are within the Socialist Republic of Serbia.

The population of Yugoslavia amounts to some 19 million people on 255,804 square kilometres. Most of the country is situated in the Balkans peninsula, while its smaller part (north of the Kupa, the Sava and the Danube) is in Central Europe.

Five Southern Slav peoples constitute the population of Yugoslavia: the Serbs, Croats, Slovenes, Macedonians, and Montenegrins. The largest national minorities in Yugoslavia are the Shiptars and Hungarians, followed by Turks, Slovaks, Bulgarians, Rumanians, Germans, Italians, Vlahs, and others. When they settled in these areas in the 6th and 7th centuries, the Southern Slavs were unaware of the fact that they occupied the most picturesque and beautiful part of Europe and they could hardly predict the price they would have to pay for this conquest. They occupied the part of Europe where the interests of all great European and Asiatic peoples would clash for centuries: Romans, Byzantines, Franks, Bulgarians, Germans, Hungarians, Turks, Saracens, Venetians, the French... All of them tried to conquer this country, if not the whole of it, then at least part of it.

The attempts of the Yugoslav people for independence and the setting up of a state of their own were frustrated for a long time. They were always separated, whether in their small states or under foreign rule. The Middle Ages passed in the creation of, at first, vassal and then independent small states. The Croats established a fairly strong state between the 9th and 11th century, only to associate themselves with Hungary in 1102 and Austria in 1527 into a personal union. Under Samuilo the Macedonians set up a powerful state in the 10th century and the Serbs created between the 11th and 14th century, especially under Dušan Silni, one of the most powerful states of those times. The disastrous defeat at Kosovo in 1389 sealed the fate of the Serbian state, only to be followed by the decline and collapse of other South Slav kingdoms and dukedoms. In the course of the 15th century the Turks conquered Serbia, Macedonia, Bosnia and Herzegovina and a considerable part of Crna Gora, reducing Croatia after the Battle of Mohacz in 1527, to the sad »remains of remains«, i. e. to the Western border country, in places not wider than thirty kilometres. The greatest part of the country was under the Turkish yoke for centuries, part of Croatia and Slovenia shared the fate of Austria-Hungary, while the towns in the littoral and the narrow coastal belt were held by Venice. The small Dubrovnik Republic was the only free and independent fragment of the Southern Slavs, it was the cradle of Croatian literature and arts. The defeats of Turks (in the 17th and 18th centuries) were followed by the expansion of Austria-Hungary and Venice which meant in fact that the Slav population in these areas only changed its rulers. Karađorđe's Uprising (at the beginning of the 19th century) meant the liberation of Serbs from Turkish rule and the setting up of an independent state that was soon to become much stronger. Only Crna Gora, on account of its impassable mountain ranges, partly succeeded in preserving its freedom.

This means that the Southern Slavs were split into several parts until the collapse of the Austro-Hungarian Empire in 1918; for about a thousand years they were mostly fighting for sheer survival.

Living separately they developed in various directions, but mainly in three cultural spheres: West European, Byzantine, and Islamic. What they had in common was suffering, the folk songs lamenting the past days of glory and keeping the hope in a better future alive. Other common factors were the folk costume, folk songs, and customs.

It is this mixture of various cultures and the rich legacy of numerous extinct cultures that makes Yugoslavia so interesting from a historical and cultural point of view. Remains of neolithic, Illyrian, Greek and Roman cultures can be found scattered all over the country.

Remains of central European culture can be found mostly in Slovenia and northern Croatia which can be seen in the numerous medieval fortifications, castles built between the 16th and 19th centuries, towers, palaces, churches and monasteries, built in the Romanesque, Gothic, Renaissance, and above all in baroque styles. The most beautiful remains come from Baroque, including buildings and whole towns. Education has an early beginning in these parts, with the Zagreb University being established in the 17th century.

The influence of Italy was felt on the whole stretch of the Adriatic coast, starting from the Slovene Littoral in the extreme north, to the Croatian Littoral, and the Montenegrin part of the coast in the south. Dozens of towns of various sizes have been preserved in this area, their existence being uninterrupted since Roman times and treasuring precious remains from each period of the past. Special mention should be made of Pula with the best preserved Roman amphitheatre, Split with the Diocletian Palace, the largest and best preserved palace of ancient times, Zadar and Rab with their rich Romanesque remains, and finally Trogir and Dubrovnik, frequently referred to as the two stone pearls of the Mediterranean. Each small town is a monument in its own right, treasuring at least several important sacral and secular buildings, mostly built in mixed styles: Romanesque-Gothic, Gothic-Renaissance, whereas the steeples and belfries preserve the Romanesque volume and decorations.

Traces of Byzantine influence can be mostly found in Serbia and Macedonia. Here we can find a considerable number of invaluable monasteries and votive churches dating from the Middle Ages, ornamented by wonderful and in many ways unique frescoes, where the anaemic mannerism of that time was abandoned for the first time, and individualised and realistic human figures were painted. The well-balanced elements, the harmony of their structure, the blending of building material, and the wealth of decorations, they all make these monasteries and churches unforgettable. The monasteries of Dečani, Manasija, the Peć Patriarchy, Sopoćani, Lazarica, Mileševo, Žiča, and others in Serbia, St. Naum, St. Nikola Šiševski, Nerezi etc. in Macedonia, the Ostrog, Cetinje and other monasteries in Montenegro, as well as the fortified towns, ranging from the Ohrid fortress to the town of Smederevo, testify to the rich and varied architecture of those times.

The lavish and picturesque Islamic buildings and monuments are scattered all over Bosnia, Herzegovina and Macedonia, part of Serbia and Crna Gora. The towers of hamams (Oriental inns) and mosques, the slim vertical lines of minarets are glittering in the sun, while middle class houses are situated all along the slopes of the hills, carefully adhering to the principle of Oriental architecture: each house has a right to a view, air and sunshine. In this Islamic atmosphere the well-known types of Macedonian and Bosnian houses were invented which exercised considerable influence on various contemporary styles in architecture. The famous Turkish roads and stone bridges are not only admired for their aesthetic features such as balance and proportion, but are still used in modern traffic. The forest of domes and minarets makes Sarajevo the largest Oriental town in Europe. Tens of smaller towns in Bosnia, Macedonia, Kosovo, Metohija, and Crna Gora complete this rich canvas of Oriental cultural remains in Yugoslavia.

Two trends of original medieval architecture developed without any external influence; they are the old Croatian chapels (built between the 9th and 11th century) and the Bogumil tombstones. It can be said that South Slavic architecture started with the old Croatian chapels (in Zadar, Nin, Split, Trogir, Omiš, Ston, etc.). The groundplan is usually in the shape of a four-part leaf, a cross, or a six-part leaf. The walls are usually built of roughly hewn stones with narrow lattice stone windows. While basilicas were covered by wooden roofs in other parts of Europe, here they had stone roofs. The Bogumil »stećci« — tombstones of extraordinary shape and size — were mostly scattered in Bosnia, Herzegovina and Croatia, and they can also be found in border areas between Serbia and Crna Gora. They are huge stone monuments of various shape and size, decorated by reliefs of knights, warriors, wild game, scenes from hunting and wars.

But the cultural and historic remains are only part of the attractions in Yugoslavia which is visited for its natural beauty by an ever larger number of tourists from all parts of the world.

Yugoslavia is one of the rare European countries which, as a whole, can be divided into two principal tourist areas: the Alpine and the Mediterranean area. While Serbia, Macedonia, Bosnia and Herzegovina attract the visitor by their picturesque countryside, thermal springs, deep gorges and ravines made by clear and rapid streams, hills and high mountains ideal for winter sports, Crna Gora attracts tourists with its stone fields, vertical rocks, mountain lakes and rivers, and with its wonderful sand beaches on the warm Adriatic. Slovenia will fascinate everybody with its wonderful Alpine countryside — which is not inferior to Switzerland — with its lakes, rapid streams and rivers, wonderful karst caves (Postojna, Škocjanska jama, Predjama, etc.) which have no rival in Europe. The mountains are ideal for mountaineering and winter sports, while a great number of modernly equipped mountain huts and resorts, thermal springs and spas, as well as the lovely coast of the northernmost part of the Adriatic make Slovenia an attractive and popular recreation area. But the most attractive part of Yugoslavia for tourists is Croatia; perhaps because out of the total length of the Adriatic (Italian, Albanian and Yugoslav), amounting to 7,867 kilometres, 6000 kilometres belong to Croatia. If we add to this major attraction the beauties of the continental part of Croatia (the karst mountain belt, the thermal springs and the Plitvice lakes) we shall understand why this republic absorbs three quarters of foreign visitors and almost one half of local tourism.

The ever better and more comfortable railway, road, and air connections with all countries in Europe, as well as the modern luxury and simple hotels, motels and camping sites attract steadily increasing numbers of tourists from all parts of Europe and elsewhere. Two important highways contribute a great deal to the growing popularity of Yugoslavia, they are the Brotherhood-Unity Highway and the Adriatic Highway. The former connects the Austrian border with Greece, touching all the more important towns in the interior of Yugoslavia, among them Ljubljana, Zagreb, Belgrade and Skopje, whereas the latter winds its way along the sunny coast of the Adriatic only to join the former road across the precipitous mountains of Crna Gora.

The purpose of this monograph is not only to make the reader acquainted with the wealth and variety of natural beauties in Yugoslavia and its treasury of cultural and historical remains, but also to present in its largest third part a picture of the life of what was once a backward people which has, however, succeeded in achieving its national and social freedom. The nation has built an efficient industry, and has given its working man modern means of production thus securing a decent way of life in his socialist country.

Ivan Raos

FATHERLAND

Even this stone of Serbia's soil
Which, threatening the sun, tears the clouds
Of the cheerless brow with sombre wrinkles,
Of remote distances is relating,
Showing with dumb mimicry
The deep furrows of its face.

These are traces of bygone ages,
These black wrinkles, the dismal gorges;
And this stone, like a pyramid
Rising from the dust to heavens,
This is a heap of ancient bones
Which in struggles against the foe
Your greatfathers have gladly yielded,
Pasting with blood of their hearts
And muscles their broken bones,
To prepare for their grandsons,
Ambushes, whence they will boldly,
Despising danger, wait for the cruel foe.

Only to this stone,
To this sturdy wall
You can tread, you heathen!
Try to go beyond, you'll hear the thunder
Through the silence of this free land
Tearing the air in horror.

You'll grasp them with fearful heart,
Speaking to you in a bold voice,
You'll hit against the hard rock
With your clean-shaven face,
In a fit of fear and anger.

But one phrase, one thought
You'll hear through the din of battle,
»This is the Serbian's native land!«

Đura Jakšić

THE MANASIJA MONASTERY, BUILT BETWEEN 1407 AND 1418. ONE OF THE NUMEROUS MEDIEVAL MONASTERIES WHICH KEPT ALIVE AND ROUSED THE PATRIOTISM OF THE SERBIAN PEOPLE OVER. A NUMBER OF CENTURIES OF HARSH TURKISH RULE IN THIS PART OF THE COUNTRY.

TO THE MOUNTAIN

Mountain, you defy time without end,
You adamantly have stood the test of time,
And when the pleasant hour returns to the earth
It will again throw upon you its youthful light.

In blossoms you watched whole nations,
In blossoms you saw their rise and fall.
You did not feel the nights of fate,
Your face still young as of old.

When in grave I shall rest
And moss will grow all over my place,
My people will enjoy their happiness
Their bright and serene days.

Then again in your fragrant dress
You will greet the vernal land,
Then, mountain, greet the youthful world,
The new generation of boys and girls.

Simon Jenko

THE KAMNIŠKO SADDLE. TAMED STONE GIANTS HELPED THE SLOVENIAN PEOPLE TO PRESERVE THEIR LANGUAGE, BUILD THEIR CULTURE
AND MATERIALIZE THEIR FREEDOM-LOVING IDEALS OVER A PERIOD OF A THOUSAND YEARS.

TEŠKOTO*

Oh, teškoto! When the hautboy's piercing shrills are
                            heard
And the drum's thunder is echoed,
Why do I then feel a smarting pain in my breast,
Why do my eyes then fill with tears,
Why do I then cry like a child
And shake mu hands to cover my face,
To bite my lips and to suppress my heart
From uttering a cry.

Oh, teškoto! Old people are coming,
Their brows are thoughtful and their eyes are wet,
And their first steps on the soft grass
Quiet and slow, with subdued sorrow.
But the drum thunders and the shrill is heard,
A lightning flashes in everyone's eye
Rushing forward and falling
Into the tightest order.

Next to old men youngsters are leaping;
Heart cannot stand it — falcon in the cage —
Writhing flame cannot stand it, dipped in the eye.
Youth cannot stand it, wanting to fly!
Here it is rocking! The earth is revolving
And you would say — the baffled world is uprooted,
And the dark hills around are trembling
Returning the echo.

The boiling ring as if grown
With the native power of this land,
In it the river is murmuring,
In it the wild and horrid world is roaring,
In it ripe corn is whispering.
A gentle even fragrance is swelling,
In its primal satiety the earth is breathing,
Throbbing with excitement.

As if all the soul of my suffering people
Had been woven into its tissue —
What has been piling for centuries
Darker than smarting pain and the cursed dungeon,
What the forceful thought has heaped for ages
On cheerful youth and the freed world,
The song — for love dying with the strains,
Like a flying crane.

Oh, teškoto! When silent I watch thee
A misty film spreads across my eyes,
All at once in an endless file
The hills are lost in hollow deserts,
Shadows are emerging from the misty dark,
Shadow after shadow, one next to the other,
In the endless file son follows his father
And grandchildren their parents.

Dark ages are its field
And their music — the screaming mortars,
Their heads to the soil are bent
And slowly they move — step after step.
On the ages my people passed in darkness
Who will find the word for your pain,
Who will find the word for the ghastly horror,
Revealing the blood and the hollow desert.

Who will tell the number of gashing wounds,
The nights in flames, the deserted ruins,
Who will call the pains gathered in your heart,
And the tears in your eyes, and the curses on your lips.
Oh, teškoto! You who were the fetters of slaves,
The string of dark-eyed girls and brides,
With hands tied, driven as captives
By the cursed tyrant.

Oh, teškoto! You who were the fetters of slaves
Until the people rose in the blossoming forests,
Until the rebellious oro ring was started,
Moved by fury amassed through ages;
Oro is rocking through flames and bloodshed,
While shouts and thunders pierce the clouds of smoke.
The rebels' feet are treading
All over the native land.

Oh, teškoto! Today when in freedom
I see the oro in our hamlets,
Is it strange — that tears are filling my eyes,
Is it strange thta sorrow I feel in my heart?
From age-long slavery, my people, you come,
But in your heart you have a golden present and a song.
Your wheat harvest will treble
And so will also your life!

* Macedonian national »Kolo« dance (Macedonian »Oro«)
                                              Blaže Koneski

ACROSS THIS ENCHANTING MACEDONIAN LANDSCAPE GALLOPED BUCEPHALUS OF ALEXANDER THE GREAT AND PRINCE MARKO'S ŠARAC, THE HORSE OF THE LEGENDARY HERO AND SYMBOL OF THE HALF-MILLENIAL FIGHT OF THE SCUTHERN SLAVS FOR FREEDOM FROM THE LONG AND MERCILESS TURKISH RULE.

THE MOUNTAIN WREATH

(extract)

The cloud has captured the sunshine,
Darkness has covered the mountain,
Before the altar wept a candle,
Strings on the fiddle were broken.
Hidden are the nymphs in rocky hollows,
Afraid of the sun and of the moonlight;
Men's breats have grown cold
In them freedom has withered,
Gone as the sun's glow forsakes the mountain crest,
Or sink beneath dark waves far down the west.
Dear God, how bright is the festival.
How the souls of our ancestors
Shall vigil hold above the town of Cetinje!
They flutter like white flocks,
Like flocks of gracious swans,
Above the surface of the shining lake.
The falcons, the five Martinovićes,
At one maternal breast all fondly nourished
And lulled to sleep by the same lullaby,
The two Novaks with Pimo, the standard-bearer,
And the knight Borilović-Vuče,
All ye who first did set upon the Turks!
Who can weave garlands to there heroes?
The memorial to your bravery is
Crna Gora and its liberty!

Petar Petrović Njegoš

DURMITOR. THESE HUNGRY ROCKS FED MONTENEGRINS FOR FIVE CENTURIES, INSPIRING THEM WITH DIGNITY AND COURAGE, GIVING THEM THE STRENGTH TO DEFEND THEMSELVES AGAINST THE FIERCE HOOVES OF THE RAVAGING TURKISH CAVALRY.

SPRING

Tonight, my loved one, do not close your eyes,
Sleep must not overwhelm you on your pillow.
While the moon smiles upon our river
An the earth is covered by silent dew

Young springtime will be born and everywhere
Scatter the scent of blue lilacs,
And like snow flakes from the boughs they will fall
Into the stream that winds through our garden.

Spring will soar high above our Mostar
And strew nosegays into all windows
To waken loving and burning hearts.

Do not, my loved one, let sleep crush you!
Come and be the first rose in the garden,
The balm to my heart till the morning.

Aleksa Šantić

WATER-MILLS NEAR JAJCE (BOSNIA). IT SEEMS AS THOUGH THEY HAVE STOOD HERE SINCE THE TIMES OF ANCIENT BOGUMILS, CALMING DOWN WITH THEIR PRESENCE THE PLAYFUL WATER, CONFORMING IT TO THE TRANQUIL OF THE WOODED HILLS.

A FORTRESS THAT DOES NOT SURRENDER

I am a fortress with only the flag of my heart.
Invisible ramparts erected by bruises,
A lullaby
Resisting invaders.
Transformed in armour of dreams,
Sentries are watching on towers, and on the coast are
                                        hidden
Boats of reed and tamarisk.
Wind cones watching remote armies of steel whetting
                                    their arrows,
Oiling their thighs and muscles, and rearing on their
                                    wicked horses
Of tin and fire.
The bridges are lifted and the irresistible torrent
Defies all approaches.
At daybreak the moon vanishes and the untroubled
                                sun shows its face.
I am a fortress with only the flag of my heart.
A fortress that does not surrender,
And the dead, freed of their senses do not surrender,
And the lightnings in their flight do not surrender,
And neither do the living with gems of their eyes.
Fortresses surrender, but not these of the dream,
They give themselves up or they resist,
I am a fortress with only the flag of my heart.

Jure Kaštelan

DUBROVNIK, CRADLE OF CROATIAN SCIENCE AND ART. ONE OF THE MOST BEAUTIFUL FORTIFIED TOWNS IN THE WORLD WHICH SUC-
CEEDED — IN THE ETERNALLY BLOODY BATTLEFIELD OF THE BALKANS — IN PRESERVING ITS FREEDOM AND INDEPENDENCE OVER A THOU-
SAND YEARS, TOGETHER WITH ITS UNIQUE ARCHITECTURE AND A GREAT NUMBER OF PRECIOUS OBJECTS FROM ALL FIELDS OF A THOUSAND
YEARS OLD MEDITERRANEAN CULTURE.

THE OLD COUNTRY

This is an old country. The deep ploughing
Is still heard, and so is the power of waters;
The growth of wilderness lifts and tears
Her injured and roughened crust.

The gorges tame the hardy roads that carry
The creaking cart and the stamping hooves.
Neglected towers on the hills remember sorrow
Of ancient soldiers, within an ell of freedom.

This is a strong country, bearded and raw;
Her not blood is carried through the veins of rivers,
Her seeds are sown by gales and rains.

This is a wild country. We look for her
Tame roots, her hidden youth
We draw from depth to the face of light.

Nikola Miličević

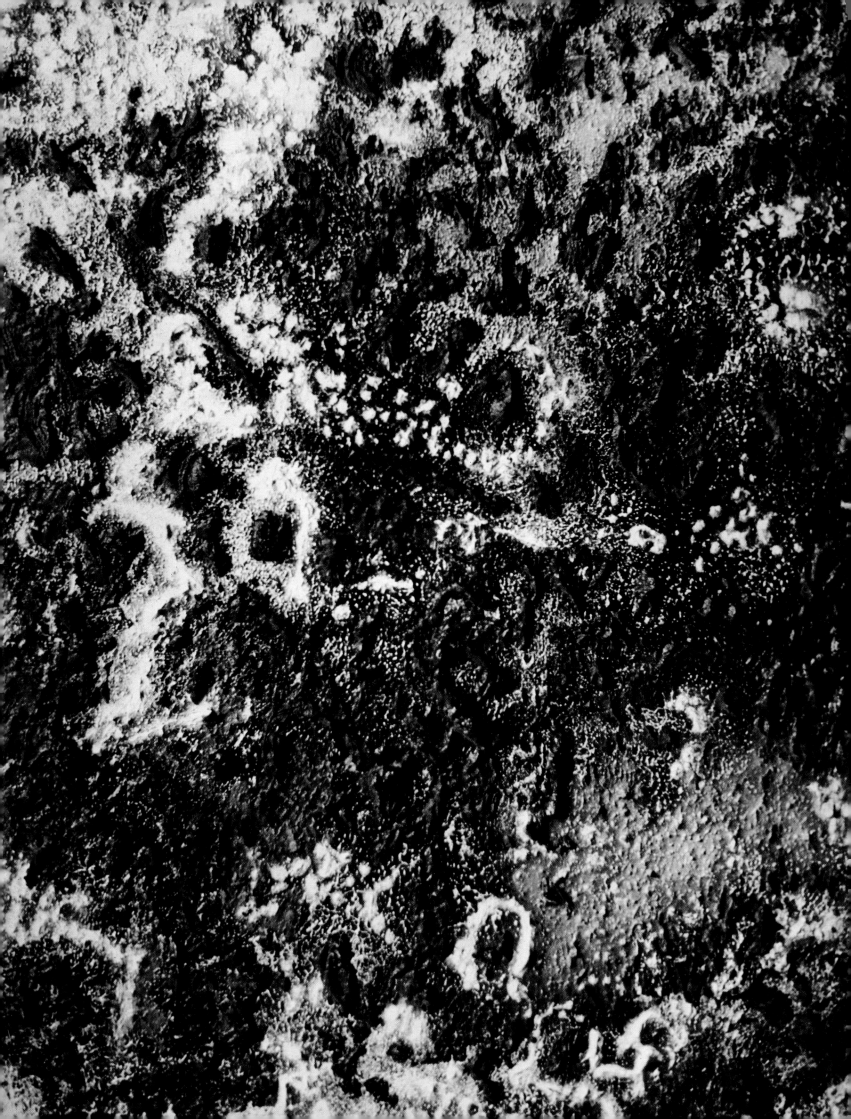

In the heart of Yugoslavia, surrounded with three republics: Montenegro, Serbia, and Croatia, lies the Republic of Bosnia and Herzegovina. Its rounded mountains, soft fields, and silver waterfalls make Bosnia alive and varied. Further towards Herzegovina the beauty of the countryside fades and merges into the scattered Karst, while the light colour of the landscape disappears among the dwarfed plants. Across centuries old Bosnian forests whose crowns stretched into the sky even in the 12th century, the Bogomils came after being cruelly persecuted in Serbia, running away from the fate of burning at the stake, and from the threatening face of Stevan Nemanja (1170-1196) their ruler of Serbia. The Bogomils rejoiced at the sight of Bosnia and hurried through its forests towards the ruler. They were welcomed by Kulin ban, who adopted their religion and made it the official one of his Court, defending the Bogomils against the Pope's Legate and promising: »We shall not accept any Manichee or other disbelievers to live with us, if we are sure that he is one; we shall stay apart from them even in the way we dress«. Bogomils found fertile ground for their work. Many times the Pope intervened, but in vain. They devoted all their attention to arranging the churchyards, neglecting the churches with their brilliant endowments. To-day the fields are still grey with the tomb-stones of that period, between the 13th and 16th centuries. People from Radimlje, Vrbljani and around Krupanj pause in front of these tomb-stones and often run their hands over carved out figures of men, admiring the scene shown of a hunt or duel. These strong heavy tomb-stones contrast with the broken ground of the Karst here in Herzegovina as a symbol of permanance. Figures of knights standing upright with crosses above their heads, or with swords beside them, as if watching over this stony area. Bosnia occupying the middle of the Balkan Way always attracted the enemy.

Under the fluttering flag with its new-moon, the Turks invaded Bosnia, forcing the enslaved to work for them and converting them to Islam. Many beautiful settlements were ravaged and destroyed, later some were better fortified by the Turks, and some even rebuilt by the side of the ruins. During their most powerful period they pulled down the old bridges and built bridges of stone with towers on each side for the guards.

Mostar, the town with dreaming minarets was once the home of Moslem wives (hanumas), who, through the window gratings looked along the streets towards the bridge over the river Neretva. Delighted with its whiteness and the reflection of the arch in the clear blue water beneath, on which the perfume of acacias was carried by a gentle wind from their gardens, they longed for the day of »teferič« when they would be allowed outside and cross this beautiful bridge. Occasionally dignitaries and viziers could be seen surrounding the creator of the bridge, Hayrudin, congratulating him for the thousandth time on the success of his single-arched bridge, which had never been built before. Evlija Čelebija, the Turkish travelwriter, spoke of its beauty and significance: »Let it be known that I, a poor and humble slave of God, Evlija, have crossed and seen 16 kingdoms, but up until now I have never seen such a high bridge«.

Under this bridge from the 16th century runs the Neretva changing its blue colour into emereld, while Mostar serenely aware of its beauty rests against the side of the mountain.

This old town, full of romance and charm, seems to be watching the new one, modern and full of lights, hotels and the rush of everyday life. Not far from Mostar, towards Nevesinje, on the bare rocks lies the broken town of Herceg Stjepan, which was destroyed by the Turks.

Because of the difficult approach to the town, only the most persistent ones manage to get there, while a greater number give up after not being able to negotiate the goat-paths. With the blocks of stone built into the bridges, the enslaved people built also their wish for the defeat of the Turks. With the largest bridge of the Turkish epoch, built in the 16th century, people connected many legends. It was built by order of the Great Vizier of Yugoslav origin, Mehmed Pasha Sokolović, and described by the famous Nobel Prize winner Ivo Andrić in his book »The Bridge on the Drina«. On this bridge with eleven arches with its duplicate reflection in the water, stood its creator, leaning against the smooth stone, looking at the verses composed by the poet, Badi, from Constantinople:

»Hear this, Mehmed Pasha the greatest among the wise and great of his time,
Fulfilled his heart's pledge and with care and effort
Built the bridge over the river Drina...
God bless this wonderful, great and most beautiful bridge«.
This last line filled him with pride more than the biggest money prize.

Along the seething whirls of this wild river Drina, glide the famous lumbermen standing upright on their rafts, wet from the foaming water which rushes along with them. On one side of the bridge stands Višegrad, huddled at the foot of a gentle hill, covered with orchards and small houses from where children bring fruit which they sell near the bridge. The river runs alongside towns with their green camping sites, forests often almost carpeted with red heather, and with cold and clear water. At the source of the river Buna the booming water rushes from a steep rock into the lake, once full of fish, which the Turks never caught because of superstition.

Not far from the town Jajce, from a rock 20 meters high, fall the rivers Pliva and Vrbas, while above their united waters scatters a spectacular show of rainbow colours in the rays of the sun. Evlija Čelebija, the previously mentioned Turkish travel-writer from the 17th century, delighted with the beauty of this waterfall, said: »Here, to sit in these green and shady places beneath the water-mills, and watch the course of the river Pliva, almost like the sea, which by the wisdom and power of God runs above our heads, and watching it cascade down the rocks, is so unique and interesting that one must admire it, and be filled with surprise and wonder.« Many travellers from abroad and Yugoslavia come to this holiday camp. Here, where once came beauties from Harems on the day of teferič, covered with black veils which were only removed from their faces at the sources of Buna and Bosna, or waterfall Pliva, where they stretched out their hands to the silver water — to-day children and adults camp, breaking the silence with their voices which overpower even the sound of water.

The entrances to the caves just above the rivers are blue. In these caves, half-blind from the dark, once hid rebel outlaws and other inhabitants, running away from the

Turks. The most beautiful cave in the Dinara Karst is Vjetre-nica on the Popovo polje. Above the town Drvar, cut into the lime-stone rock and framed by green undergrowth, can be found the historical cave with its little fairy-tale house in which Tito hid during the drop of German paratroops on Drvar on 25th May 1943.

The largest mosque in the Balkans is Gazi-Husrev Begova Džamija, in Sarajevo. Built with the money plundered in wars during the 16th century, this mosque seems out of place among these old streets by the market-place. Its interior is decorated with wooden carvings. In the court--yard is the grave of Husrev Beg, its founder. Near the mosque, along Baščaršija which was restored after the great fire, one can find little silversmith shops in which copper and silver gleam in the hands of the craftsmen. With the ringing noise of the hammer beating out the metal, the reflection on it from the sun dazzles the buyers. Wonderful cases, cigarette holders, and women's bracelet charms lie piled up in the shop windows of these small work-shops covered with red tiles. In every street there is a craftsman of one sort. Near the Teferič fountain in a small square, old people meet to talk. From aščinica, the small cafés spread the smell of popular dishes along the street, while the sellers, with their long colourful pipes (chibouks) pass the time watching the clouds of smoke.

The visitor usually pauses near Husrev Begova Medresa, built in the 16th century from finely dressed stone, and admires the doors in the facade which is regarded as one of the most beautiful portals of Osmanli architecture in these parts. It bears the following inscription: »Meeting place of benefactors, Home of the perfectionist«.

Aladži džamija in the town Foča was considered by Evlija Čelebija to have no competitor, neither in Bosnia, nor in Zvornik Sanjak or anywhere else. In the court-yards of these mosques one can find drinking fountains, many of which decorate small towns. Still to-day women move along the narrow streets with pitchers of water. On his way through Sarajevo Evlija noticed a great many of these fountains. He said: »According to the words of a knowledge able man of Sarajevo, this beautiful town has one thousand and sixty fresh springs and wells, but let him bear the responsibility of his words«. It is clear that Evlija himself suspected the accuracy of this remark.

The all-consuming fire which swept Bosnia along under the Turkish flag, gave way before the Austrian invaders. During the Austrian Régime Bosnia suffered the same fate as when under the Turks, only in place of the new-moon which faded away, the threat came from the dark eagles on the new flag. The great Yugoslav writer, Petar Kočić, in his work »Badger on Trial« showed a picture of the impover-ished peasant of that time. These words full of sarcasm, »thank you, honourable Judge, for relieving me of my load« helped the rising awareness of the people to their plight. Young writers from Mostar showed this revolt against injustice.

A row of bridges join the banks of the river Miljacka. On one of these echo the foot-steps of Gavrilo Princip, a young patriot, who from that bridge killed the Austrian heir and so caused the fall of the Austro-Hungarian Régime. Not far from there is the museum of Gavrilo Princip. From various photographs one can follow the course of the trial. The members of »Young Bosnia« sit one beside the other calmly following the trial, without sign of repentance for what had happened. In one of the photographs can be seen Princip's parents dressed in rich national costumes, proud and at the same time sad because of what had happened and won-dering what fate awaits their son.

Two different cultures of the invaders intermingle in Bosnia. In architecture we can see the influence of the east and the west, reflected in the styles of building over the centuries. After the first invaders small towns remained with gardens full of the strong scent of flowers, lovers' meeting-places near the bridges, wells and fountains in the yards and by the road-side. The next invaders left behind them massive buildings, roads, and baths. As to habits, the former instilled indolence towards life and apathy, and from the latter administration and bureaucracy without limit was learned. A long time ago many taverns in Bosnia and Herzegovina vanished. One of the last, han Morić in Sarajevo, is slowly falling into decay. Beautiful hotels with pools full of fish attract the traveller. Newly built roads seem to have gathered on them many small houses. From the doorway of these houses one can step directly on the road, while from the back one can go down trought the green field to reach the river or brook.

Zenica, to-day a modern town, once was a settlement in whose vicinity on the Bilino polje in the 12th century Kulin ban solemnly rejected the Bogomil faith. Large furnaces, steel--works and other objects complete this large industrial town in to-day's Yugoslavia. Thousands of workers pass by with their shadows on the river of molten metal.

Along the white roads of wooded Bosnia and under the trees with their intermingled crowns, rush coaches full of trippers who go to the spa Ilidža and the source of river Bosnia, occasionally stopping in small exotic towns.

The town of Jajce, in which the last Bosnian King Stevan Tomašević in the 15th century received a crown ornamented with glowing emeralds as green as Bosnia itself, and the place where he was assassinated three years later, attracts many visitors. In Jajce one can see the museum in which one of the greatest dates in the history of Yugoslavia is recorded, the second meeting of the Anti-fascist Council of National Liberation of Yugoslavia (29th — 30th November, 1943) which laid the foundations for new Yugoslavia.

Green are the rivers with thick forests growing along the banks which scatter their leaves over the water flowing towards the estuaries. The most famous of these rivers is the Sutjeska which with its softly flowing water honours the fighters who died there, while stone slabs record the names of heroes who fell for the sake of liberty, and the children who to-day happily wave to people passing by.

Nebojša Tomašević

In this largest and most populated Republic of Yugoslavia, the interchanging plains and hills going towards the south finish with wooded mountainous country. Narrow paths lead near the fenced-in orchards, through whose branches, blue with plums, peep the roofs of houses, while vineyards stretch along the undulating hills. Over the fields of Vojvodina, and those near the rivers Danube, Sava and Morava, big and strong stalks of corn stagger under the weight of their heavy yield. Streams and brooklets, whose water reaches every meadow, wrestle with the ploughed earth, and disappear into it, only to suddenly burst out again rushing towards the first river expanding its water. Serbia first became important in the 12th century with the Dynasty founder, Stevan Nemanja. His heir, Stevan Dušan, from the same Dynasty Nemanjić, made Serbia the strongest state in the Balkans. At Nemanja's heirs' court tables were set with gold and silver dishes, and toasts were made with golden goblets ornamented with precious stones. The two-headed eagle in the middle of the silver plates bordered by Czar Dušan's name, defying the wear of centuries, still exists in the same pose with his wings together, in a glass case in the National Museum of Belgrade. The gold leaves which fell, nobody knows why, from the binding of the Gospel from the 12th century, lie nearby.

In those days Serbia was admired by the rest of the world for its richness, especially with respect to its mines. In his report to the French King Guillaume Adam wrote (in the year 1332): »Serbia has five gold-mines, and five silver, where miners work continuously. Whoever wins over this country will acquire a beautiful ornament, the most precious of this century.«

Monasteries are spread over the whole country, which were gifts from Nemanjić Dynasty: for example Dečani, Sopoćani, Manasija, Žiča, and others give evidence of the high culture and ingenuity of that period, whose frescoes to-day arouse the curiosity and acknowledgement of the whole world. With the charters in respect of presented land from the ruler to the monasteries, also came gifts and golden articles. From the richly ornamented iconostasis the pious faces of saints look, contrasting their placid faces with the dazzling frames. In the 14th century the bells rang very often in these royal endowments announcing the coming of the Osmanli Turks. From the holy walls Stevan Nemanja anxiously watched his ancestors squabbling, making it up, and then ending by fighting against the Turks on Kosovo. Under the leadership of Duke Lazar in 1389 the cream of the nobles of that time went to the Kosovo field to stop the invaders. The whole of the Christian world in central Europe alertly folowed the battle, waiting for the outcome. An army, three times greater than the Serbian one, was waiting on the field of Kosovo. The greatest hero of that dying Serbia was Miloš Obilić, who went to greet the Sultan Murad and in front of the eyes of his triumphant guards, instead of kissing the Sultan's slipper slashed open his stomach with a dagger. There is not a historian who doesn't know of his name. Even the Turkish travel-writer from the 17th century Evlija Čelebija, mixing truth with legend acknowledged the deed of that brave man: »After the battle the disbeliever stepped forward as a messenger to kiss the hand of the Padishah, drew out a dagger, killed Han Gazi Murad, and jumped on a horse and ran away«. A large number of soldiers shot at him with various guns, but nobody managed to hit him. One feeble old woman said: »Hey, warriors, aim at his horse because he is in armour and you can't hurt him. And when they had killed his horse he fell and perished«. On hearing that a Serbian Duke had killed the Sultan Murad, and mistakenly concluding that the Serbs had won, some European countries celebrated that illusive victory with long ringing of bells. Among the first was the Notre Dame Cathedral in Paris, which rang to the victory of Christian arms. The bells trembled for the dead on Kosovo. And what good men fell »Praise to Kosovo« tells us, which was supposedly written by Despot . . . Stevan, the son of the dead Duke Lazar. »There were good people there, brave people, people true in word and deed, who shone like bright stars in their golden armour ornamented with precious stones, like the ground patterned with flowers«.

By the wish of Duchess Milica, the wife of the killed Duke, the rest of the Serbian knights gathered together all the arms of the deceased (shields, spears and sabres) and from part of this they cast a black candlestick, and together with two big candles sent it to the most beautiful monastery of medieval Serbian architecture — Dečani.

Murad's tomb still stands on the deserted field of Kosovo (where the Sultan's intestines are buried). Its neglected appearance in the 17th century infuriated Pasha Melek Ahmed, who ordered the natives in the vicinity to clean it and build a wall around it with a gate, to dig a well and to post a guard there who could look after the carpet of silk, candlesticks, the incensories and the containers with oil of roses. From the hard ground of the Kosovo field, almost at every step peeps out a stone which marks the grave of a dead Turk. The deserted, round tomb seems as if held together by three of four scanty trees with which it is surrounded. This place, where once Turkish nobles and people used to come, nowadays from time to time is visited by inquisitive tourists who stop for a moment to see this rectangular stony monument with its inscription of the battle of Kosovo. This monument dominating the field remains in their memories for a long time, as well as the beautiful monastery Dečani, built in the 14th century, which with its red-white marble walls can be seen from far away. This endowment of Stevan Dečanski, with its richly elaborated windows and portals standing out from the smooth stony walls, is the most preserved and most beautiful monastery from Medieval Serbia. On the wall inside spreads an ancestral tree of the Nemanjić Dynasty. From the Dynasty founder Stevan, came good and bad, strong and weak, descendants. Above the door the figures of the father and son seem to approach each other, the father, Stevan Dečanski seems to have an expression of forgiveness, while the son, Czar Dušan as if asking forgiveness because of keeping his father in captivity until death. A golden-blue colour richly enhances the gowns of the saints, and above these there are innumerable figures and compositions created by national artists in the style of Byzantine, while high up on the arched ceiling is a painting of the head of Christ Pantokrator watching over the saints. Visitors who bend back their heads look into Christ's eyes. Over the black candlestick, which was a present from the Duchess, is a thin layer of green patina.

Travelling in these parts the tourist can see high chimneys of the old and new mines which reach up towards the sky: Trepča, Janjevi, and others known for the production of lead, which take the first place in Europe. These mines bring together the population of this area, wiping out every difference in belief and nationality for the first time in the history of these people.

Around Prizren, once the capital of Serbia, stretch green vineyard plantations. The craftsmen from Prizren, well-known even in the days of Nemanjić, produce unusual effects with gold and silver wire used for filigree-work. Ear-rings in the form of pagodas, bracelets of tangled snakes with eyes of blood-red coral, buckles in beaten silver; all of which are in demand throughout the world.

Among the gardens full of the fragrant smell of the quinces, and tall mulberry trees, walk women with long heavy hair, so like the girls in the frescoes in the church of the Virgin Mary Ljeviška, built in the 14th century. For centuries the beauty of these frescoes was preserved under a layer of plaster, which was put there by the Turks to transform the building into a mosque. But many other monasteries perished during this time. Manasija, a monastery built in the 15th century, which was an endowment of Stevan the Despot (the most intellectual medieval Serbian ruler) was unavoidably robbed. After the fall of the Serbian state the monastery in turn served the Turkish and then the Austrian garrisons. Where at one time the voices of the monks could be heard praying, and where the holy texts were copied, now stood warriors with bare swords on the monastery walls, watching the Serbian slaves dying with their blood running towards them.

Beside the river Danube still to-day can be found ruined medieval fortresses. It takes one a long time to walk around the walls of Smederevo town, which was built in the 15th century. The story handed down from ancestors to posterity was that all people from the district, although only living on bread, were forced to work. People were convinced that Despot's wife, a foreigner, was to be blamed for this hard work and called her »damned Jerina«. Because of damage from explosions and bombardments during the last World War, occasionally a tower is missing from the wall. In the cellars of Smederevo town, not far from its walls, in barrels of 2,000 litres, the best wine in Serbia ferments. Further along the Danube on the hills arise the military settlements Golubac and Ram (14th and 15th century). Tower after tower stretch up the hillside linked together by a wall. It is understandable why the Prussian officer Otto Dubislav Pirch admired these towns on his way through. Having climbed up the hill with great difficulty, and exposing himself to danger, he reached the town of Golubac and wrote: »One is filled with awe at the courage of these people who on this ridge built such a massive wall«. Later, desribing the towers, he emphasised: »High towers on both ends of the wall, and with the Danube on the two sides, almost directly beneath me in the depth below, made such an impression on me that I was completely rewarded for all my effort«.

Situated behind Golubac is the most beautiful gorge in Europe: Đerdap. At this place the Danube suddenly narrows between sheer rocks. On one side of this gorge an inscription was made referring to the building of a road during the time of the Roman Emperor Trajan (1st century A. D.). Once long ago, steersmen of the boats paid with their lives the journey through the fast water of the gorge. To-day — (in fact the walls were built as a defence against the Turks) ships take passengers on the most beautiful tours to see the unique gorge.

From Avala, a mountain near Belgrade, (where once was situated a medieval town called Žrnov), and where now stands a monument to the Unknown Soldier, one can see a large part of Serbia. Softly undulating hills, scattered with villages, stretch as far as the eye can see, while on the other side of the Sava in the distance stretches the cornfield of Yugoslavia, Vojvodina. In the main town of Vojvodina, Novi Sad, there is the oldest institution of Serbian culture, »Matica srpska«, with a gallery of old Serbian paintings of Vojvodina. In the immediate vicinity of this gallery there is a large modern building called Beljanski Gallery, where the works of the best Yugoslav painters, belonging to the time between the two wars, are shown. Recent paintings are also on display.

It is uncommon for a foreigner who visits Belgrade not to wish to see Avala. The monument to the Unknown Soldier, which stands on the top of this mountain, was made by the famous Yugoslav sculptor, Ivan Meštrović. The eight figures on the monument are really women in national costumes from all provinces.

From Avala the road begins to drop and twist towards Belgrade, the main town of Serbia, and the capital of the whole of Yugoslavia. Evlija Čelebija, comparing it to a diamond ring, once said that Belgrade had been the ideal which prompted aggressive aspiration of many countries.

In Serbian museums, especially in the »National Belgrade Museum«, many old Greek and Roman excavated objects lie, which were found near Vinča, Vranj, Ripanj and other places. Golden masks, coins, stones and signet-rings stand in line, as witnesses of the people who passed through this country. These objects were not found only by archaeological excavations, but were found, and still are found to-day by peasants ploughing their fields.

In the »National Belgrade Museum« there is a mask which belonged to Czar Konstantin, found in the vicinity of Niš, and it stands witness to the highly developed culture of the people who made it. Near this town the Ćele-kula can be seen. In its walls are 57 rows of heads of Serbian patriots (built after the battle of Kamenica in 1809) through which the water runs and pours down the tower almost telling of the savagery and barbarity of the invading Turks. Horrified at this sight the great French poet Lamartine dedicated his most beautiful verses to this tower. Embittered subjects without rights started a rebellion. During the rebellion the Turks shut themselves in the mosques in the stronghold in Belgrade, of which a large part is still to-day standing. Words on the well of the old Mehmed Pasha Sokolović: »Come here my bey, if you wish in this world to drink from a heavenly spring, Ab-u-hajat« in vain encouraged the Osmanli Turks. But they preferred to go down the flight of steps to the old Roman well (still there to-day) to get water, leaving the public springs to water the dry land.

From Kalemegdan spreads a wonderful view of the rivers Sava and Danube.

The most modern air-port in the Balkans is in Belgrade, receiving passengers from all parts of the world. In 1945 Belgrade had 250,000 inhabitants, which in the last 20 years has grown to one million. Now it is a town lit by neon lights, with modern buildings, and completely new part joined to the old part by a long modern bridge.

Nebojša Tomašević

Because of its nature Slovenia is an exceptionally attractive country for the tourist. Ivan Cankar, the greatest Slovenian writer, didn't call it »the sky under the Triglav« without a reason, and for the famous Slovenian poet Prešern, the part of Slovenia — Gorenjsko — was »a picture of the sky«. It is a country which excels in variety and brilliant colours. A large part of Slovenia is covered with the east and west Julian Alps, which are known throughout the world for their extraordinary beauty. Another part of Slovenia, Pohorje, is on a branch of the central Alps. One can also find wide rocky areas, near the sea, which is one of the most beautiful parts of the northern Adriatic coast, mountains and hills abundant with medicinal mineral waters. The furthest north--eastern part stretches as far as the Pannonian Plain. All this is gathered together in a comparatively small space of 20,000 square kilometres: the sea, Karst, hills, mountains, and plains. This small part of Yugoslavia is varied, rich, sensational, impressive and like a lyrically calm festival of natural beauties, which in an interesting way blend together with many valuable monuments of Mediterranean and Pannonian culture (artistic, ethnographical, urban, archeological, historical etc.).

The Slovenian coast covers thirty kilometres along the sea--shore from Ankaran to Piran and Portorož. There one can see all the bizarre beauty which is characteristic of the western side of Istra: Mediterranean blue sky and sea touching green gardens full of wine stocks and early vegetables. All houses are built in a typical low Mediterranean style, forming picturesque groups around interesting church steeples, and all shaped so as to blend with the landscape. A gentle climate guarantees a pleasant holiday in every season of the year. 26—28 centigrade in summer, with an average sea temperature of 22 centigrade. In autumn the sea is warmer than the air. The average temperature in January is 4.5 centigrade.

Ankaran, Koper, Izola, Strunjan, Piran and Portorož, are the main tourist centres which offer all facilities.

The tourist centre in the Slovenian Karst is Postojna, in whose vicinity is situated the famous Postojna Cave, which every year draws about 400,000 visitors. Near Postojna Cave there is a whole row of caves, which because of their specific wonders are included among the most interesting caves in the world: Škocjanska jama, Predjama, Križna jama, Pivka jama, are only a few of the numerous marvels which the Slovenian Karst displays to its visitors.

Snežnik, Vremščica, Nanos, Javornik, Trstelj and Slavnik are mountains which make a wonderful background to the northern Adriatic and Trieste Bay, contrasting with the scattered villages, pine forests, archeological and palaeontological monuments. All this can be easily reached from the tourist centre in Postojna.

Under the Triglav mountain lies the pearl of Slovenia. Dr. Julius Kugy, world propagandist of the Julian Alps, referred to it as the »Triglav Kingdom«, including Bled, Bohinj, all Gorenjsko and Gornje Posočje. The Slovenian Alps, east and west Julian Alps, Kamniške Alps and Karavanke with their forms, flora and fauna, rivers and lakes, thrill us with their harmony of colour, as well as with their fantastically shaped peaks, out of which the highest is Triglav (2,863 metres). Triglav is a unique Alpine peak, ending with one of the highest and steepest rocks in the Alps. It has interesting surroundings with mountain ridges and green slopes.

Soča, whose source comes from under Jalovec, is from Trenta to Tolmin the most beautiful Alpine river. Lake Bohinj and Lake Bled set in mountainous surroundings are the most picturesque Alpine areas. Other places of interest are: Jezer-sko with Kočnami and Krok, Kamnik with Grintavec and Bistrica, Solčava with Logarska dolina, Kranj with Storžič an Križna gora, Radovljica with Begunjščica, Stol with Dobrča, Kranjska gora with the hidden Pišnic in the shadow of the gigantic Prisojnik and impressive Razorje. It is almost impossible to count and describe all these places. All this should be seen to believe what the World Alpinists say, that the Slovenian Alps, with their resorts, are a unique Alpine area.

Recently many facilities have been built, in particular ski-lifts which helps the development of winter sports and tourism throughout the year. Vogel, Komna, and all the Bohinj mountains, Krvavec with Grebenom, Velika planina and others, offer special enjoyments to the skiers, due to the fact that these areas have not, so far, been transformed into modern playgrounds, which definitely diminishes the feeling of contact with nature, so necessary for the present man. Pohorje in particular is appreciated, with its sea of green forests in summer, and in winter covered with a strange calmness on the snowy roads. At the same height as Pohorje a mountainous world stretches from Gorica and Vipava up to Tolmin, Podbrda, Škofja Loka and Logatac. There are less known geographical names such as: Trnovski gozd, Idrijsko and Cerkljansko, Rakitovec, Porezen, Blegaš, Jelovica and Sorška dolina, rich with a whole range of natural beauties, as well as with ethnographic, urban, historical, archeological, and other valuable places of interest. One who has never looked from the top of Vojsko or Jelenec, and has never seen Poldanovac, Crni vrh, central Hrušice and Idrian surroundings has no idea of the beauty and cultural richness concentrated on the western border of Slovenia. What innumerable beauties can be discovered by the tourist in these mountain villages: Sorica. Prtovč, Davča, Stržišče in the vicinity of Črno prstjo!

All mountains which are accessible are supplied with ordinary mountain huts (160 huts accommodating 5,000). All are connected by the Slovenian Mountain Transversal from Maribor to Ankaran, which is becoming more and more well--known abroad.

The heart of Slovenia is Ljubljana, its economic, political and cultural centre, with monuments showing the course of history from before the Roman times. Numerable pretty holiday camps around Ljubljana give it the characteristics of a tourist centre.

To the south comes Barje with Krim, Iškim Vintgar, Mokrcem and Krvava peć, then Rakitna, Bistra and Pekla. To the north there are Šmarna gora, Rašica, Polhovgradec, Toško čelo with Osredkom, and to the west comes Janče, Lipoglav, and across the Sava the old Vače.

Looking from Ljubljana across the picturesque Zasavlje we can see Celjska kotlina with all its beauty. In the distance the white peaks of the Savinjske Alps, and the vivid beauty of the Gornja Savinjska dolina, Pohorje and Konjiška gora, are visible. The southern horizon reflects the profile of the Zasavlje hills, and the undulating relief of the Planinsko — Kozjansko area — beautiful, wine-growing country. Nature gave the district around Celje many medicinal mineral sources which are well-known outside the borders of Slovenia. Rogaška Slatina is the most famous and most visited, enhanced by the impressive heights of Boča, Stražnik and Donačka gora. Another mineral source, Dobrna, is hidden more or less from view. Laško and Rimske Toplice, are warm mineral waters which spring from the bottom of the surrounding mountains: Tovst, the pointed Hum, Kozje, Lisca with Bohorje, Kopitnik, and the impressive Šmohor with Maličem. Each mountain is beautiful and attractive in its own way. A traveller wishing for a change of scenery can cross Socka in Šaleška dolina, to arrive among big buildings of the modern town Velenje, where on the rich deposits of lignite this town seemed to grow up overnight. If one takes the road along the palaeontological Huda luknja, he will arrive in the area of Koruška, which in the year 1918 was joined to Yugoslavia, and still to-day with the mountains Pec and Kralj Matijaš as a symbol of Slovenian countryside on its northern border. Crossing Kobansko and Maribor one can arrive in east Slovenia, with Preko-murje beneath the mountains and hills characteristic of the whole of Slovenia. Lovers of this kind of country will find the same thing in Dolenjsko and Bijela Krajina, where the country climbs to Gorjance, and further on to the magnificent Rog with Mirna gora, ending with the height above Bloški plateau.

There is no place in Slovenia that has not been given some of beauty, of shape, volume or colour, which together with people's handicraft, makes always something well worth seeing.

Tine Orel

CROATIA

Through areas once covered by the calm depths of the Pannonian Sea now run the wide dreamy waters of — Savus, Dravus, Danuvius — on which float boats and rafts with tourist steamers and motor boats. Quietly dreaming at the bottom of this dead sea are the shelters of the Neanderthal man, neolithic and Illyric settlements, ruined towns of old Rome — Andautonia, Siscia, Mursa. Above their ruins to-day wail factory sirens and sound automobile horns, in the towns of Zagreb, Sisak, and Osijek. And many towns and villages have sprung up on this enchanted land of the two seas: the dead Pannonian Sea, which in prehistoric times withdrew its cold water, leaving behind the rich and fertile Pannonian Plain, and the live Adriatic Sea with its warm restless water still wearing away the mountains, forming calm little coves and regularly covering them with fresh carpets of even whiter and finer pebbles and sand.

Between these two seas spreads the grand Karst mountain mass: one moment with bare inaccessible cliffs, the next moment mountainous slopes with impenetrable centuries-old forests, glades and hollows, valleys and ravines, funnel-shaped holes and miniature valleys, plateaus and pathways, bottomless pits and a strange rocky network of underground caves, green Karst rivers and white foaming streams, glaciers and mysterious transparent and cold mountain lakes.

The country of Croatia is a country of the two seas: the live Adriatic and the dead Pannonian, and two confluences of rivers: flowing into the Black Sea and the Adritic, two unique natural beauties: one of the bluest and most indented coast of the world and Karst rivers with rich barriers of gypsum.

Two influences in culture: Mediterranean and middle-European. And in the end, two big European tourist-recreative zones: mountainous and Mediterranean.

Besides the Pannonian Plain — which because of its rivers rich with fish, low-lying and swampy areas, and an abundance of varied game, is one of the tourist-recreative areas — the whole of the continental Croatia represents a distinctive mountainous tourist-recreative zone. In the heart of the Pannonian Plain rise the wooded Slavonian hills, like a gay necklace surrounding the fertile and rich valleys. Centuries old oak forests with picturesque hills, lakes and streams, mountain hotels and camps, and pools with cold and thermal medicinal waters, as if created for special rest in relative solitude and calmness, so badly needed in this mechanized age.

The country in which the last mountain-spur of the Alps meets the most western inlet of the dried out Pannonian Sea, is the most romantic area of Croatia. This well-known, sung about, and painted, Croatian Zagorje, is situated immediately at the back of Zagreb, the main town of Croatia. »Beautiful hills or green...« And green and blue, yellow and ruddy, like ochre and terracotta, thousands, and thousands of various coloured areas (forests and meadows vineyards and orchards, pastures and fields) harmoniously blend in one inseparable whole. As though a great artist spread a huge colourific canvas over the whole area. Besides unique landscapes and monuments of cultural and historical value, one can find here rich hunting grounds and warm medicinal waters, which were known and used even by old Romans. Many of the centurions, and perhaps a great army leader once bathed in Varaždinske, Krapinske, Stubičke, and Tuheljske Spas.

On the southern side of the wooded mountain Medvednica, from which a hundred kilometres of wonderful landscape can be seen, and at the edge of the dried Pannonian Sea is situated the free Royal Town of Zagreb (Charter of 1242). Around two Medieval fortified settlements — possibly built in the 10th century — developed a modern town of 500,000 inhabitants, which is a political, social, and cultural centre of Croatia, and also the biggest industrial and transit town of Yugoslavia. Woods and water are two of the basic geographic characteristics of this town and its near and far surroundings. Medvednica with its unusual vegetation abruptly slopes down the back of the town, and with its wooded hills reaches to the very heart of the town, and up to the edge of the main traffic artery. As a contrast to this splash of green, and complementing it, stands the river Sava with its lakes and pools, and well-organised bathing places. Further away from Zagreb, within a semi-circle with a radius of fifty kilometres — from the Slovenian border across the Samoborsko gorje, Plješivica, Banija and Kordun, as far as the estuary of the rivers Una and Sava — woods and water especially figure, offering great possibilities for a range of sporting activities: mountaineering, kayak canoeing, rowing, swimming, hunting, fishing, and all winter sports. In the south-west of this area Gorski Kotar is situated, which best of all represents a mountainous tourist-recreative zone. Scattered mountain ranges, mostly covered with dense forests inhabited by various kinds of wild life, sometimes uncover themselves to expose wonderful slopes for all kinds of winter sports, sometimes in the form of peaks climbing high into the sky and tempting mountaineers and alpinists. Occasionally they crowd together enclosing the water of fascinating mountain lakes, and in places they break up to allow the mountain streams through, in which live the eternally attractive world of fish. At a height of over 700 meters a number of tourist places are situated, as well as holiday resorts and convalescent homes, while the mountain huts and camps are at a height of over 1,000 metres. A fresh mountain climate, within easy reach of the sea and good communications, make this country convenient for various outings.

In the middle of Croatia, in the Karst valley between the mountains Mala Kapela and Lička Plješivica, is situated one of the greatest natural rarities in Europe: the sixteen Plitvice Lakes, formed from the united Crna and Bijela rivers and the Ljeskovac brook. The lakes lie like steps, and the water cascades from one into the other over gigantic barriers of gypsum. These barriers never get any smaller, on the contrary they constantly grow, because milliards of microscopic organisms in the water form this gypsum. These Plitvice barriers with their marvellous shapes, waterfalls up to 70 metres high, large and small caves, meanders and other attractions, offer the eye a complete kaleidoscope of unimaginable beauty. The lakes blend with forests of high beech trees and darkgreen conifers, which occasionally preserve the appearance of primeval forest, in which still hides the lonely brown bear — the keeper of the forest and this enchanted wilderness. The whole area of the Plitvice Lakes has been proclaimed a National Park.

Parallel with the Adriatic coast, on the other side of the chain of mountains Velebit-Mosor-Biokovo, runs the barren Karst Lika and Dalmatinska Zagora. These high deserted Karst plateaus, like the rough surface of the moon, with pitiful undergrowth and bushes, sharp grass and sparse fields, mysterious funnel-shaped holes in whose depths one can glimpse blue water — tranquil and menacing, dried up river-beds vertically cut through the rock by the once alive rivers, as well as running water at the bottom of canyons, and the porous calciferous structure of the mountains with numerous caves and holes — all these things give an unusual charm to this unique country. The Mediterranean zone encircles the Croatian coast (Istra, Hrvatsko Primorje and Dalmatia), one of the most interesting and indented in the world. The exceptional type of coast in Dalmatia is well known not only to a geographer, but to ordinary European citizens. 526 kilometres of air-line between the two farthest points of the coast, cross over the actual coast-line of 1,778 kilometres. If we add 1,185 islands and islets, with their circumference of about 4,200 kilometres, we have almost 6,000 kilometres of coast-line (approximately the distance from London to New York, or from Paris to Bombay!) in fact it makes 76% of the whole Adriatic coast-line, including parts out of Croatia. When we know this fact, then it's not difficult to understand why Croatia — though covering only 21.1% of the area of Yugoslavia — takes three quarters of the foreign, and almost half of home tourism.

The rather low and grassy shore of the western Istra soon changes to high and steep mountain chains, which in places sweep down to the water, occasionally standing away from the sea leaving behind narrow strips of land. The sea wears its way into valleys between the mountains, as well as into lower sliding parts of the plains. In places this penetration of the sea is wider and deeper, making big and spacious bays (Kvarner, Bakarski, Šibenski and Kaštelanski, Novigradsko and Karinsko more, Neretvanski and Stonski kanal). Occasionally the sea creates longer and narrower inlets, making fiords (Limski kanal, Zavrtnica). On the whole of this continental and insular coast, as well as in these bays and fiords, one can find big and small rocky, pebbly, and sandy coves and beaches, and natural and artificial ports. Not a kilometre of straight coast. From the extreme north-west to the furthest south-eastern point meanders this unique coast, and along it runs the Adriatic Highway, which cut through the grey Karst rock, crosses a line of towns and villages, of which many have something from their neolithic, Illyric, or Roman history (Pula, Rijeka, Zadar, Split, Trogir, Hvar, Dubrovnik etc).

It is interesting to see the way in which the islands are scattered. The Istrian coast is mostly surrounded by uninhabited islets. The only inhabited ones are those of Brioni. In the Kvarner area a few of the larger islands are: Krk, Cres, Lošinj. The nearer one gets to the middle Adriatic, the islands and island-groups become closer and closer together and more disconnected from the coast-line. One of these island-groups, Kornati (125 islands, islets and rocks) seem to emerge like precious stones from the blue depths of the open sea. Towards the south islands become infrequent and larger, after which they again get smaller until in the far south they change into deserted rocks.

From the climatic point of view there is a remarkable difference between the north and south Adriatic. The nearer you approach the south from the north, the sea becomes warmer and saltier, the air becomes moistureless and overcast skies and showers rarer and rarer. For this reason Dubrovnik and the Elafitski islands and surroundings have more hours of sunshine during the summer months, than any other town in Europe, so being equal to Alexandria. The same change occurs with the green scenery. The peaks and masses of the Karst mountains are almost entirely bare, except for the miniature bushes and sparse grass, while the belt along the coast is green with Mediterranean woods (pine, cypress, jasmine) or undergrowth, Mediterranean grass and cultivated areas. And again, the more one travels from the north towards the south, more and more orchards and vineyards can be seen, with pomegranates, olives, lemons, oranges, and palm-trees and oleanders. The grass and bushes have a stronger scent, and the pinegroves are thicker.

With the building of the Adriatic Highway the influx of tourists from Central Europe has been enlarged. This inevitably affects the growth of the existing tourist facilities and the creation of new ones. Along the whole Adriatic coast one can find hotels and motels, pensions, hostels, holiday camps, other camps and various sports facilities. The coast is intensively urbanized. And in a few years' time the whole of the Adriatic coast will be joined in one united colony, a holiday resort 2,000 kilometers long!

In the introduction we mentioned that one part of Croatia was influenced by Central European culture, while the other half was influenced by the culture of the Mediterranean. In order to understand why the culture of one small country should have split into two ways, it is necessary to know that Croatia was for centuries politically divided. In the 8th century the heart of the Croatian State was formed with its centre round the ruins of the old Roman Salone. Under Tomislav, at the beginning of the 10th century, the country became a kingdom, widening its borders as far north as the rivers Drava and Mura, and it represented an important political, military and naval power. Croatia was strong and powerful as long as she was ruled by kings of national origin. In the year 1102 a pact was made with Hungary which united the two countries, and they shared the same government until the battle of Mohač in 1526. After 1527 Hungary and Croatia joined with Austria in a new union, and so remained within the borders of the Austrian Kingdom up until 1918, when the Monarchy fell and the South Slavs formed a new national state.

If we bear in mind how Mediterranean countries quickly recovered from the heavy blow which was brought about by the migration of people, and the fact that the South Slav accepted Christianity and with it the culture of the Mediterranean world, long before the north, then it is understandable that Zagreb first became known only six years before the pact with Hungary in 1102. Up until this decisive year the Croats from the coastal area erected many basilicas and churches, dukes' and kings' castles and a whole line of cultural-historical monuments, built in the well-known style of old-Croatian architecture. It should be pointed out that the largest number of pre-Romanesque monuments were built here on the Adriatic Coast. All these things, thanks to the sea, which is the best, the safest, and the fastest road which has always helped to connect peoples and cultures.

During the turbulent Middle Ages — with the invasion of the Mongols, piracy, Crusades, and large and small wars — it was not possible to form, let alone improve, cultural unity with the north. Furthermore, in 1409 Vladislav Napuljac sold Dalmatia to the Venetian Republic, under whose government it remained until Napoleon. During this time (four centuries) it was separated from the rest of Croatia which suffered greater misfortune under the blow of the Osmanli sabre. At the beginning of the 16th century the Turks penetrated far into the west and reduced Croatia to a sad »remains of the remains«, military belt, which in places was no wider than 30 kilometres. It is true to say that this battle lasted daily over a period of two centuries, and in such conditions the Muses seldom showed any sign of themselves, let alone sing.

The war crushed and destroyed all. That is why in Zagreb and the whole northern part of Croatia one can find only the very remains of pre-Romanesque and Romanesque churches and monasteries, citadels, castles, fortified towers and towns. Somewhat better preserved are the citadels and towers from the late Medieval ages, built to oppose the invasion of the Osmanli 'world' in Europe. Among the ruins very well preserved parts of fortified architecture can be found, in particular those from the 16th and 17th centuries. Gothic style arrived very late and left a few arches, windows and portals. In the central Karst area there are quite a number of ruined medieval towers and strongholds, abounding with traces of old-Croatian, old-Christian, late-Antique, Antique, and Illyric culture — and in the end quite a collection of high tomb stones (stećci), which are occasionally quite rough, or finely carved and decorated. With the wars came a period of passivity, with literature, art and science becoming stifled in the tumult of battles, and the old monuments smashed into mere ruins.

After this age of passivity bright facades of sacred and secular buildings sprang up, with their many gay vertical lines in harmony with their domes. The luxurious interiors glittered with gold-plated wood and polished stone. Baroque! Baroque in this case didn't mean just the style of the victorious counter-Reformation, but was the optimistic outlook towards the future of the people who, for centuries without a pause, were bleeding in battle against the Turks along the military line of several hundred kilometres. At last the Turks were pushed back to the other side of the Una and Sava, and culture could commence!

Architecture is accompanied by other fields of science and art. The important writers appeared, together with historians and linguists, who all together paved the way for the National Renaissance in the 19th century. Slowly music as an art developed, with dramatic literature and theatrical art. In the 19th century the University the Academy of Science and Art was founded in Zagreb, as well as many museums and galleries. It should be mentioned that Zagreb has the largest collection of Glagolitic manuscripts in the world, Museum of Typhlology, unique in Europe, a mummy with the longest Etruscan text, remains of the skull of the Neanderthal man

(homo Krapiniensis), so that one can get an idea of the richness of material culture, preserved in approximately 30 museums in this town.

It has already been mentioned that Baroque was prevalent in Zagreb, as well as in the north of Croatia, while some towns to this day are almost completely Baroque in style (i. e. Varaždin). Many churches in Hrvatsko Zagorje and Posavina, besides many castles and courts, many public and private halls in town centres, were built in this style. The interior of the church in Belec, St. Katarina, and Rauch's palace in Zagreb, are only reflections of hundreds of Baroque buildings erected all over north Croatia.

And the classicism in these areas left quite a number of valuable, mostly secular buildings, castles, public and private halls, and town houses. The largest number of sacred and secular buildings were built in so-called historic styles. As in Central Europe these sacred buildings were predominantly built in neo-Gothic style, and secular buildings in neo--Renaissance and neo-Baroque. According to the opinion of Loos and Wagner, Zagreb is among the first towns in Europe to build in the spirit of modern architecture.

The cultural-historical monuments in the coastal area of Croatia are far more numerous and varied than those in the north. This fact is not due to quicker and immediate influences from over the sea, nor to the relative security from Turkish invasion, but to the fact that these monuments were found by Croats on their arrival in this advanced area of the Roman Empire. Although the Croats with their wild allies, the Mongols, succeeded to destroy many Roman towns, they did not demolish all the monuments of Roman and Greek culture.

Still to-day in Pula stands one of the best preserved Roman amphitheatres, and in Split can be found the intact Temple of Jupiter, the Mausoleum and cellars situated inside the well--preserved walls of the colossal and unique Diocletian Palace, the ruins of Salona and Narona, and hundreds of sculptures and sarcophagi deposited in museums. One could almost say that wherever one digs, traces of old Romans, Greeks or Illyrians, and perhaps of neolithic man, could be found.

Barbarians destroyed the Roman Empire, but became enslaved by its culture. This enslavement first appeared on the Adriatic coast. With the swords hardly put back into the sheaths, they began building late-Antique monuments, and already started the unique basilica in Poreč.

Athough the influence from the Apennines, Byzantium and Frankish areas was very strong, the newly arrived Croats did not entirely submit, and when they did, they brought in their own artistic feeling. While the west European builders of basilicas were covering them with wooden roofs, in Croatia they were being vaulted. Late-Antique decorations were changed into pre-Romanesque, and pre-Romanesque churches were decorated with foliaged sculptures. Lacking the means to build luxurious buildings, they built as they knew and could. In this way old-Croatian architecture was created. The ground-plan of these buildings was cruciform or circular, with 3 or more apses. The walls were built from roughly dressed stone, finished with an arched roof (i. e. small churches in Zadar, Nin, Split, Trogir, Omiš and Ston). These buildings are regarded as being some of the oldest monuments of all Slavs.

From the 11th to the 13th century many Romanesque churches and monasteries were erected, and to this day many are preserved, such as: Cathedral in Zadar, Rab, Trogir, the churches of St. Marija and St. Krševan in Zadar etc. On the Croatian coast Romanesque left numerous wonderful buildings.

While in the north of Croatia Baroque perpendicular style dominated, on the coast Romanesque steeples absolutely ruled. Whether built during the 11th or the 19th centuries, they were always built in Romanesque style. Although on some of them the elements of Romanesque, Gothic and Renaissance are combined together, even whole storeys, Romanesque predominates with its firm and heavy form, and closed distinct lines.

This Romanesque perpendicular style and central paved square represents the basic urbanistic core around which the towns are shaped. Strongholds and ramparts form the border of a town. Even when the ramparts are pulled down (many are preserved almost completely up until to-day), and when the town expands with its developing industry and with sky-scrapers climbing up into the sky, its paved square and Romanesque steeple always remain its centre. Split is a living example of this.

Late Gothic and Renaissance affected almost every little town on the coast, and in many of them left wonderful monuments. It is enough then to mention the Šibenik Cathedral, and the Rector's Palace and Franciscan Monastery in Dubrovnik. Beside objects of sacred architecture rise the high ones of secular character: ramparts and towers, strongholds and commoners, in all towns large and small, on the Dalmatian coast. The fortified architecture of Dubrovnik, Korčula, Trogir and Hvar still to-day fills one with admiration and wonder.

The remarkable characteristic of coastal architecture is a harmonious combination of styles. Most frequently Renaissance is mixed with flowery Gothic, in the form of an attached Gothic storey to the Renaissance base, and quite often Romanesque mixed with Gothic, as well as a combination of Gothic, Renaissance and Baroque. Dubrovnik is the best example of this intermingling of styles, as one of the most beautiful stone structures in the world. Each one of these numerous towns, large and small, is in itself a small museum representing a thousand year development of Croatian architecture, like a little pearl in the wonderful stony necklace of the Croatian coast.

There is not enough room here to describe them in detail. It is sufficient to say that, since the arrival of the Croats on this coast, and up until to-day, culture has always been present, continuously being expanded and revived, that European attainments were always reflected in Croatia on time, that many national artists and scientists, outside the borders of their country, created and succeeded to place a stone in the general building of culture, that even in the Middle Ages sculpture and painting existed alongside architectural monuments, with valuable carvings in wood and precious metals, that already in the 15th and 16th centuries the lively and rich artistic word, written in Croatian, flourished and that this very coast was the cradle of the Croatian State and culture, and that this culture has continually been improved and enriched.

In the end it can all be condensed in one sentence: the country of sunshine and sea, exceptional natural beauties and valuable cultural-historical monuments, the country which should be seen and experienced.

Ivan Raos

MACEDONIA

Like a beautiful carpet woven from the valleys and grey mountains spreading towards Albania, with the golden threads of rivers reflecting the sunshine, stretches Macedonia in the south-east of Yugoslavia.

Beneath mountain cliffs near crowded settlements, are silver springs in which Macedonian women with folded up skirts whiten their linen. Hands wave to and fro with the wet linen which, with rythmic strokes on the rock, echo down the valley, and the women bending over remind one of frozen white birds which in vain spread their wings for flight. Only for a moment do they stop working with their arms in the wide sleeves to greet the curious on-lookers who come to the beautiful lakes and springs, and stop on their way to the old town-walls where on the ruins they can conjure up a picture of the past.

The springs near the town of Ohrid are exceptionally beautiful, and are mentioned in folk-songs. Stone-paved roads led to the old towns of Macedonia such as Kratovo, Prilep, Prespa, Skopje and others known in history under other names, past the squares, taverns and fountains where the traveller could rest and refresh with the cold water. Smail the First, a Macedonian Czar from the 10th century liked the town of Ohrid, which in those days was the centre of Slavic culture, and he moved his throne from Prespa to this town. From the top of the hill the Czar admired the dreamlike and transparent Lake Ohrid, while the sky above reflected its blue colour in the lake full of trout and eels whose supple bodies glided by in shoals without end. On the hill above Ohrid still stand the white ruins of Smail town. It still reminds one of the glory and defeat of the first Macedonian Czar, who collapsed and died at the sight of his soldiers crippled by the wild Czar Vasilije II from Bulgaria, who captured and blinded (on the mountain Belasica) fourteen thousand soldiers, leaving to every hundredth one eye to lead the others back to their Czar. Lake Ohrid sleeps 700 metres above the level of the sea, and wakens only with the tides, while the tower of stone with its semi-circular apertures watches over it.

Still to-day, looking at Ohrid's steep streets and oriental appearance, one can conjure up a picture of the past which bears the mark of old invaders. In front of the houses in the doorways old people sit wearing dark red fez caps, so like the poppies from the Macedonian fields. Near the entrance to the mosque believers' shoes stand in rows. While the muezzin sings, the eyes of the latecomers lift up to the minaret and the strong voice hurries them along. There is a beautiful combination of air and water and a refreshing breeze under a sun which can burn, although one is quite unaware of its strength.

In the dusk old fishermen mend their nets, while the boats with bringht lanterns glide through the night. The words of a song about a poor emigrant who didn't return home say: »A curse on the country which separated me from my dearest«, seem to heavily hang over them like the lead in their nets which sink to the depths of the lake.

This beautiful Dojransko lake, on which one can still see the traditional way of fishing, keeps flocks of diving-birds which rush after the fish disturbing the calm water. Even Herod of Greece wrote about the lake. The travel-writer Ivanić, because of this remarkable method of fishing was so impressed that he described it in detail: »we went along the bank of the lake until we came to the fishermen's settlement which is a row of huts made of reeds, firmly fastened down with strong poles. When I climbed one of the roofs I saw a fenced space down in the water where many birds were floating. They were put there for the purpose of diving under the water and driving the fish into the stretched net and hurdles, from which the fishermen take them.« ...»these birds are the right hand of the fishermen on the Polinsko-Dojransko lake«. Embraced by the range of Belasica mountains, lies this lake rich with unusual sorts of fish, which once supplied Skopje, Solun and even Serbia.

At one time Macedonia was exclusively an agricultural country. And to-day on its lush pastures one can see herds of sheep guarded by Sharplaninian sheep-dogs, trained to fight off the wolves if necessary. The tops of the mountains Galičnik and Šara are white with flocks of sheep, and the fields of Đevđelija and Pelagonija are of a rusty-brown colour from the tobacco which is drying in the sun, threaded in rows and waiting to be taken to one of the numerous factories in Macedonia. In the heat of a sub-tropical summer especially suitable for a good yield the ripe pouches of cotton open, after which the pickers industriously pile them in their baskets. The Macedonian peasant enjoys the view of the rice growing in Kočanska kotlina and Pelagonija. At one time these fields were not cultivated. Because of loss of land to the enemy, and stricken by poverty brought upon them due to unfertile land, the Macedonians left their land and went abroad to work. Only in songs were they able to return home to their families, and with sad melodies they expressed nostalgia for their abandoned land. Limited to a small space for living in those days of invasions, their folklore was also influenced by the same restriction. With the sounds of a smooth drum, almost on the same spot the Macedonian begins to dance, firstly carefully and later quicker and quicker but always with restrained agility, expressing a wish for freedom and love. This talented people for music and folklore created an outlet in art for which he was free. National costumes, richly embroidered with soft colours are regarded as some of the most beautiful in Yugoslavia. Often during invasions the costumes for the Macedonian women were enlarged by sashes and petticoats which gave their slim figures a bigger appearance, thereby saving them from the enemy. In spite of the weight of this costume the women wore it with grace.

Wood-carvers from Debar were famous for their iconostasis and had no competitors in their craft. The iconostasis in the church of St. Spas is a witness of their skill, and to this day is the most beautiful in the Balkans. Another iconostasis of special value is to be found in the monastery Lesnovo on which two-headed eagles stand decorated with sacred marks, and with wide open wooden eyes waiting for a call. Numerous churches and monasteries beautify Macedonia. They stand as symbols of the mighty past or glory, and were erected by the kings who presented them to the saints or to the towns, for the redemption of sins of for new victories. These churches and monasteries to this day still preserve the images of their founders.

On the south bank of Ohrid Lake stands the monastery of St. Naum from the 10th century. It was built by St. Naum, the brother of Kliment Ohridski, who as Metodije's pupil was owed so much gratitude by Macedonia, for the work of education and spreading of literacy among Slavs. Around the monastery is a low wall and fence which guards the tombs of the dead, and among them is the tomb of the great Educator. Under the weeping willows sitting at tables, the visitors absorb the tranquil atmosphere of the Monastery.

One can see in the distance the line evenly cut through the undergrowth which leads to the frontier post which separates Yugoslavia from Albania.

In the heart of Ohrid is the church of St. Sofija, a beauty among churches, which was saved by the Turks from destruction because of its beautiful lines, and they transformed it into a mosque appealing to Allah instead of the Christian God. It was erected in the second quarter of the 11th century by Archbishop Leon, and on its wall can be seen pictures from three different ages. In front of the fragments of the old marble iconostasis and monumental pulpit with canopy, the visitor pauses filled with inexpressible admiration. Rising up on the wall is the slender figure of the Virgin Mary surrounded with the saints who intently watch her ascend. The Samuilo's Empire had periods of deterioration and restoration but during the reign of King Milutin of Serbia (13th century) and Czar Dušan The Powerful (14th century) it was born again. The talented painters of icons imprinted along the walls of churches the images of the powerful Czar Dušan and his peers. His might was, as noted by the Greek, Gregor, without limit. »The Serbian King looked upon the Grecian wars as an opportunity to enlarge his kingdom, and as an all consuming fire he took hold of towns one by one, country by country, and there was nobody to stop him«. From the walls of the monastery Lesnovo, near Kratovo, looks the hard warrior face of the Czar staring somewhere to the side, expressing the strength of all his people. By his side is the Czarina, proud of her Czar for introducing Law into the country. The Czar's clothes glow with precious stones woven into the material, together with a two-headed eagle. The great Duke and founder of the church of St. Gavrilo in Lesnovo, is painted a little lower down than the Czar's family, carefully holding the church in his hand. Beside him is the fine face of his wife, showing the profound line of her nose and small mouth set with an aristocratic appearance. The whole of the religious world is gathered on the walls of the monastery, from Archangel Gabriel with the strong hair which was common in that era, to Juda the betrayer, rushing to meet his visitor. The even cross built into the foundations of the church, is repeated, as in a mirror, in the roof. Near Staro Nagoričane there is the church of St. Đorđe, restored by King Milutin in 1313. In this church on the stony floor, with rapt expression, surrounded by his retinue, knelt the Serbian King Stevan Dečanski praying to God on his way to Velbužde (to-day Ćustendil) where a great victory awaited him. And here at the same place, he fulfilled the wish of the crying enslaved Bulgarian knights and gave over the body of their dead King Mihailo. These words of Archbishop Danilo show us an age of chivalry, in which there was a place for dead enemies: »and our Lord King, having heard their wish, spoke with his peers and so ordered that the body of the Czar be taken with honour and laid in the church of St. Mučenik Georgije near a small place called Nagoričkoga«. On a great area of the walls Saints die in pain. Partly on the wall but mostly on the pillars the church calendar is illustrated for the whole year; month by month in correct order.

Nearby the capital of Macedonia, Skopje, which before the earthquake in 1963 was full of beautiful monuments and relics, stands the Monastery Nerezi. Judging by the ordinary exterior of this monastery from the 12th century, one would never expect to see such a display of beauty and value. On the fresco — mourning after Christ — is the Virgin Mary embracing the strong lifeless body of Christ with an unusual and sincere expression of sorrow, which is rarely seen on frescoes from that time. This beautiful monastery with the church was dedicated to St. Panteleimon, set apart from the road, and seems to absorb the calm of the valley.

Macedonia attracted many writers and explorers with its strange beauty and folklore. To-day as a change from before, the inhabitants of Macedonia work in factories and their songs now have a happier tone. No longer is their enjoyment and entertainment only walks as during the time of Ivanić, in particular Bey-bašta, Kiosk-bašta. The habit of group marriages among the young people (Galička) which was for a long time usual before leaving for work in foreign countries is dying out. Macedonians are again bringing Skopje back to life from the ruins (for the third time destroyed by earthquake). Now, quicker than ever before, houses are being built one against the other, piling the roofs towards the sky.

Nebojša Tomašević

MONTENEGRO

Montenegro is situated in the south-eastern part of the map of Yugoslavia, and seems to slope towards the sea. The peaks of the bluish mountains appear to be enveloped in mist. In the grey Karst and in the mist above it, are woven stories of the honour and courage of the mountaineers. Even in the days of Njegoš, the great Bishop-ruler and writer, this country attracted visitors from foreign countries. In spite of the fact that the Austrian Regime in those days disturbed and tried to discourage these visitors, they still came eagerly and later wrote about their experiences. Edward Mitford wrote in his notes: »After all those dangers with which they tried to frighten us in Kotor, it was really enjoy-able for us to have friendly relations with this foreign head--man and his tribesmen«. And the Saxon King Frederick August II, who had been Njegoš's guest, wrote in his diary: »...a guest has nothing to be afraid of with Montenegrins«. The visitors came on foot along the meandering horse-paths, or on horses, admiring the landscape and people. Like a precious jewel the mountain Lovćen would suddenly emerge from the mist in front of them. This mountain so delighted Njegoš that he expressed the wish to be buried in a tomb on the top of it. The sheer grey cliffs glowing like sabres, wonder-ful and dangerous at the same time, tempted the visitors to climb higher and higher, until at last a marvellous view is spread before their eyes. Almost on a line with the sky, in the distance the blue of the Skadar Lake can be seen, and the surrounding hills covering the green vineyards evoke the wish to be there. Thrilled with this scene, almost out of this world, Edward Mitford wrote in his notes: »From the highest peaks we had a wide view over to the Skadar Lake and the Albanian mountains, which spread far away in the south--east in one glorious panorama.« Through grey areas twist little paths without an end while the loose stones give way under the feet making still more difficult the already inacces-sible settlements. Writing about Montenegro the great French writer, Pierre Loti said: »Eight days have gone by since my arrival. Little by little I got used to these huge rocks«. From this we can guess that this vast rocky landscape made a strong impression on him.
What was it that pushed Montenegrins to climb these bare rocky mountains. This typical building of settlements in Montenegro was influenced, more than in any other European country, by necessity rather than economic reasons. Only governed by the wish to escape the enemy they chose such places high up, or from where one could easily see the approaching enemy. They deprived themselves of better living conditions, fighting with nature in their stony settlements with hardly any water or soil, which in fact they had to carry on their backs, laboriously making their tiny fields fenced in with stones.
Whole rows of these stone walls spread over the hills and arouse the interest of the passer-by. Long processions of women, after the sunset, carrying barrels of water on their backs disperse along the paths leading towards the scattered houses where the thirsty inhabitants wait for them. This sort of life naturally left a mark on the Montenegrins. Thin, muscular, and used to walking over the rugged rocks, which so surprised Frederick August that he wrote in his diary: »With unbelievable easiness these people move over danger-ous rocky paths. To go over the steep mountain sides from rock to rock, above crevices, means to them the same thing as when we walk along the straight street«. Of course, in those days one could never imagine a Montenegrin without arms, and the Austrian King with understanding concluded: »These crude mountaineers are already, because of their way of life, from early youth used to all physical endurance. And so they should be excellent shooters, because their boys of six years already get guns in their hands.« The way in which Montenegrins carried their rifles worried the King, who later said: »I had less confidence when I saw the way in which they carried their rifles, whose barrels were pointed exactly towards my face, and it was even more unpleasant because these people never shoot blindly. Quite a usual position for a rest was to carry the rifle over the shoulders with the arms thrown over it«.
The mountains used to echo with the sound of salvos in honour of the occasional guest, or in battle against the centuries old enemy the Turks, who come even as far as Cetinje. Then the echo from the hills contrasted with the flames from the burning town. On the charred ruins and with stones taken from the surrounding hills, an even more beautiful Cetinje has been built, which for many years has been the capital of this proud and small country. And to-day after hundreds of years the white Cetinje Monastery is still attached to the cliff. In a box of velvet, instead of a medal for bravery, lies a war trophy, the head of Mehmed Pasha Skadarski. The guest closes his eyes, but the image of the executed head persists. In the lower rooms of the monastery there was a printing-works, which Njegoš proudly used to show to his guests. Here his book »Hermit of Cetinje« was printed. In this monastery to-day is preserved the first printed book of the South Slav, »Oktoih«, which was printed in Obod in 1493. Obod is situated above the little picturesque town Rijeka Crnojevića, and the first printing-works was brought there by the Crnojević dynasty less than 20 years after the first printing-works in Europe. To-day under the arches of the monastery and under the flag-stones lie the Montenegrin rulers and members of their families. Later rulers lived more luxurious lives than Njegoš. In the castle of the last King Nikola Petrović, nowadays the museum of Montenegro, visitors can see wonderful furniture, rooms with wood--carvings, expensive vases, collections of antique arms, countless flags snatched from the enemy, paintings of scowling Montenegrin Dukes, famous for their bravery in wars. All these rooms are kept exactly as if the owners have gone for a walk in the park and could come back any moment.

Njegoš's portrait, the work of the Vienna artist Johann Bass, seems to bid goodbye to the visitor.

In what better places could one imagine the past but in these monasteries scattered over the Montenegrin mountains and inaccessible gorges. The monastery in Ostrog, gleaming among the rocks, is more like a stronghold than a temple. As if the maker, stopping for a quick breather, leaned it against the rock and forgot about it. One foreign tourist referred to it as the place to which it is easier to fly than walk. At the source of the transparent river Piva is a monastery. The people who live in the district talk about the legend in which it is said that the Turks spared this monastery many times supposedly because a figure of one of the founders on the frescoes represents the Turkish Pasha Sokolović. Richer than other monasteries, often presented with icons and rich robes, this one was for a long time under the protection of the Russian Czar (until the revolution in October 1917). Built in the 16th century by the patriarch Savatije it educated many famous religious personalities. To-day one can find there a large number of well preserved and important frescoes. On the fresco Nemanja, the St. Simeon Mirotočivi stands with his thin intensive face seemingly listening to the river Piva, as if waiting for the believers who ask to be healed.

In the dense forests north of Kolašin, Nemanja's grandson, the Serbian Duke Stevan, built the monastery Morača. The synodic church, dedicated to the Virgin Mary, is really a basilica with a dome and a low transept. The portals are built in Roman style. Pictures represent different scenes from legends. On the façade of this church one can see wild horses carrying St. George. The church of St. Nikola is also situated in the same Monastery. On the walls outside are the figures of saints with dry expressions, and above the entrance door a protective roof.

Wonderful lakes like mountain eyes beautify Durmitor, the highest mountain in the Dinara Range, rich with pastures and forests. The sky softly blends with the two glittering lakes which are surrounded with sheer rocks rising above them.

The traveller's eyes glance along the high mountain ridges finding out the entrances to caves. In time of war, even during the last one, many of these caves successfully hid the ill, wounded, or healthy, and altogether equally dangerous for the enemy. Possibly fear was the reason why the Fascists filled in one of the most beautiful caves in Montenegro, Lipska pećina, near the village Dobrsko which is close to Cetinje. There stalagmites and stalactites like luxurious crystal chandeliers glitter and sparkle in the water of this underground lake. After the war this cave was excavated and now is an attractive place for visitors.

This slender bridge over the wild river Lever Tara, which was destroyed during the war by its creator, young engineer Jauković, has now been reconstructed with its original six arches. Captured by the enemy he was shot at the entrance of the bridge, which he had built with pride, destroyed without regret, and died there.

The climate along the Montenegrin coast is sub-tropical, while directly above the mountains are snow covered. The peaks of Prokletije are overspread with everlasting snow which give the appearance of heads with white turbans.

Recently the Adriatic Highway began to cross this Karst area, cutting through the Canyon Morača, and near the small historical monastery Savina built in the 14th century. Little towns on the coast, for instance, Herceg-Novi, Kotor, Budva, Ulcinj — surrounded by walls which climb towards the mountains, are, during the summers, full with tourists, from Yugoslavia and abroad. Here one can find the dead town of Perast, whose inhabitants once were famous sea-men. Nearby the white road which leads to the town stands the castle of Pivljanin Bajo, a national hero, who waited on the mountain Vrtijeljca with a company of three hundred, for an army of thirty thousand Turks in 1685. He fell, together with his three hundred friends, cut by Turkish sabres, in the defence of Cetinje, the town he loved so much. To-day Montenegro, with something more than 400 thousand inhabitants, represents one of the six Yugoslav Republics. Due to the effort of its people and to the help from the other Republics it is rapidly changing from a backward into a modern country.

Nebojša Tomašević

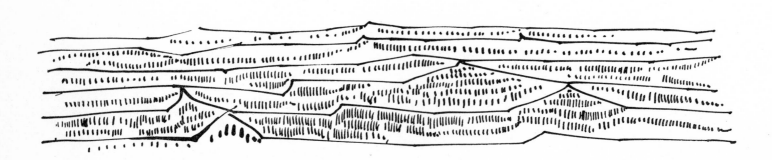

»STEĆAK« — MEDIEVAL TOMBSTONE, FROM THE RADIMLJE NECROPOLIS. MOST »STEĆCI« CAN BE FOUND IN BOSNIA, HERZEGOVINA AND CROATIA. IN ADDITION TO OTHER ORNAMENTS THESE TOMBSTONES ARE DECORATED BY RELIEFS OF ANIMALS, WILD GAME, FIGURES OF KNIGHTS, WAR AND HUNTING SCENES. MOVING INSCRIPTIONS REACH US LIKE EXPRESSIONS OF FEAR AND ANXIETY: »...DO NOT TOUCH MY LEGS, BROTHERS AND GENTLEMEN, DO NOT MOVE MY BONES«, »...I LAY DOWN A LONG TIME AGO AND HERE I SHALL LIE FOR A VERY LONG TIME«, ETC.

RUINS OF STEPANGRAD. BY AND LARGE MEDIEVAL CASTLES AND FORTRESSES IN BOSNIA AND HERZEGOVINA WERE BUILT BETWEEN THE 12TH AND 15TH CENTURIES. THEY WERE BUILT IN PLACES WHERE TWO RIVERS WOULD MEET, ON PEAKS OF HILLS, SURROUNDED BY TWO OR EVEN THREE ROWS OF WALLS, AND FORTIFIED AT THE BEGINNING BY SQUARE AND LATER OCTAGONAL OR ROUND TOWERS — IN THOSE TIMES PRACTICALLY IMPREGNABLE, EVEN FOR LARGER ARMIES.

MILJEVINE NEAR FOČA. IT IS NOT EASY TO FIND ANY LANDSCAPE IN THE WORLD THAT WOULD NOT HAVE ITS — EVEN IF IN SMALL PROPORTIONS — COUNTERPART IN YUGOSLAVIA. HAVE NOT THESE ROCKS BEEN TAKEN FROM A WESTERN OR IS IT NOT THE CRATER OF A VOLCANO? IF WE FORGET THE POOR VEGETATION, DOES IT NOT REMIND US OF THE RIDGES OF THE DEAD AND WASTE CRATERS IN THE MOON?

THE NERETVA RIVER VALLEY. FOR TENS OF THOUSANDS OF YEARS FIERCE KARST WATERS HAVE BEEN MELTING AND CARRYING AWAY THE LIMESTONE, CUTTING ROMANTIC VALLEYS INTO THE VERY HEART OF MOUNTAINS. THEN MAN CAME AND CUT A PATH ON EITHER SIDE OF THE CANYON PATHS, THUS LINKING — AS ONLY MAN CAN DO — THE USEFUL WITH THE PLEASANT.

NOTHING BUT WASTE GREY ROCKS. AND YET, IN THIS BARREN LAND OF HERZEGOVINA, AMONG ROCKS SCORCHED BY SUNSHINE, GREEN BLADES OF GRASS CAN BE FOUND WHICH FEED SHEEP, THE ONLY WEALTH OF THESE MOUNTAIN PEOPLE WHO ARE TEMPERED BY LONG STRUGGLES FOR SURVIVAL AND FREEDOM.

SHARP RIDGES OF STONE FIELDS TURN INTO GENTLE CURVES, SQUARE SHAPES ARE SUBSTITUTED BY OVAL ONES, AND THE STONE DESERT BY LUSCIOUS MEADOWS AND DENSE, FRAGRANT CONIFER TREE WOODS.

IT WOULD BE FAR MORE USEFUL TO BUILD A STRAIGHT ROAD. BUT . . . WOULD NOT THAT SPOIL THIS WONDERFUL PLAY OF LINES, THIS HARMONY OF SHAPES AND GENTLE HILLS WICH DO NOT SEEM TO BELONG TO THE EARTH, BUT LOOK AS IF THEY WERE FLOATING AND SWINGING IN SERENE AUTUMN WEATHER. VERY OFTEN MAN SACRIFICES WHAT IS FUNCTIONALLY BEST FOR WHAT IS MORE BEAUTIFUL.

THE WATERFALLS OF THE KRČICA RIVER CRUSH INTO THIS GLASS COBWEB. THE WHITE FOAM AMONG THE RUGGED ROCKS ROUSED POPULAR IMAGINATION TO STORIES OF WHITE MOUNTAIN FAIRIES AND THEIR DISHEVELLED HAIR WHICH HAVE BEEN HELPING THE PEOPLE TO FIGHT AGAINST THE FORCES OF DARKNESS FOR CENTURIES. VERY OFTEN THEY HAVE ALSO HELPED OUR PEOPLE TO FIGHT AGAINST RUTHLESS INVADERS AND THEIR ATTEMPTS TO CONQUER THE COUNTRY AND DESTROY ITS PEOPLE.

THE KRVAVICA RIVER WATERFALLS. HIGH AND IMPRESSIVE SEMICIRCULAR BARRIERS FORM ON MANY RIVERS MAGNIFICENT WATER-FALLS WHERE MASSES OF WATER CRUSH AND CALM DOWN IN A PEACEFUL SMALL LAKE ONLY TO CONTINUE THEIR BOISTEROUS FLOW. ON EITHER SIDE OF THE WATERFALL THERE ARE SHOALS OF SILVER TROUT, ATTRACTING ANGLERS FROM ALL PARTS OF THE WORLD.

THE KUPRES FIELD. LIKE AN OLD CANVAS WITH DEEP LAYERS OF GYPSUM AND COLOUR. PEACEFULLY. QUIETLY. AS IF STILL WAITING FOR TIRED CARAVANS TO REST IN THESE QUARTERS FROM THE 18th CENTURY. AND HOW MUCH HUMAN BLOOD WAS SPILLED HERE ONLY IN THE SECOND WORLD WAR IN THE DAUNTLESS FIGHT AGAINST HITLER'S FORCES.

THE VITOROG MOUNTAIN. THE SHARPLY DIVIDED STONE STRATA ARE TELLING THE STORY OF THE RUTHLESS WAR THAT THE SUR-
FACE OF THE EARTH IS WAGING WITH ITSELF, WHILE THE GREY ROCKS SING A BALLAD ON THE INNOCENT DROPS THAT ARE SLOWLY
REMOVING EVEN THE LAST CRUMBS OF SOIL, MELTING IT FINALLY AND RETURNING IT TO THE SEA FROM WHICH IT EMERGED.

SPRING OF THE BUNA.
SPRINGS, ABOVE ALL THESE WILD SPRINGS AT THE FOOT OF STEEP AND BARREN ROCKS, HAVE ALWAYS ATTRACTED MAN WHO, WHILE
RETURNING TO THEM — SOMEWHERE AT THE BOTTOM OF HIS HEART — THOUGHT THAT HE WAS RETURNING TO THE SPRING OF
HIS LIFE: THE DRINK OF REJUVENATION IN ALL STORIES WAS NEARLY ALWAYS SOME MYSTERIOUS SPRING; IN ALL RELIGIONS
ALMOST ALL ENCHANTED PLACES WERE TO BE FOUND NEXT TO SOME SPRING. A SPRING ... IS SOMEWHAT MYSTERIOUS.

MOSTAR. IN THE SPACIOUS KARST VALLEY IN HERZEGOVINA, ON THE FAST SILVERY NERETVA, THIS OLD TOWN IS SITUATED. THE
TOWN IS NOT ONLY KNOWN FOR ITS EXCELLENT WINE AND TOBACCO, BUT ALSO FOR ITS FAMOUS BRIDGE AND OTHER BUILDINGS
DATING FROM THE BEGINNINGS OF TURKISH RULE (15th to 17th CENTURY).

THE TURKISH BRIDGE ACROSS THE DRINA AT VIŠEGRAD (16th CENTURY). IVO ANDRIĆ, THE NOBEL PRIZE WINNER, TOOK THIS AS THE CENTRE OF HIS FAMOUS CHRONICLE »THE BRIDGE ACROSS THE DRINA«, WHERE PEOPLE, THE MILIEU AND ATMOSPHERE OF A SMALL BOSNIAN TOWN IN THE COURSE OF SEVERAL CENTURIES OF TURKISH RULE ARE DEPICTED WITH GREAT ARTISTIC POWER.

SARAJEVO. A UNIQUE ORIENTAL TOWN IN EUROPE. A TOWN OF CUPOLAS, MOSQUES, MINARETS, BATHS AND »HAMAMS« (OLD TURKISH QUARTERS). RICH IN CULTURAL AND HISTORICAL SIGHTS FROM ROMAN TIMES (ILIDŽA) AND THE BEGINNINGS OF TURKISH RULE (15th CENTURY). LUSCIOUS VEGETATION, WONDERFUL MOUNTAION LANDSCAPES, VANTAGE POINST, MEADOWS, RIVERS, AND THERMAL SPRINGS
... AS IF EACH PART OF BOSNIA GAVE A PRESENT TO ITS CAPITAL.

THE DUVANJSKO FIELD. LIKE A MAD CRESCENDO, FIELD FOLLOWS FIELD, ONE FOREST AFTER ANOTHER, HILL NEXT TO ANOTHER HILL — ALL OF IT ACCOMPANIED BY ROARING RIVERS AND WATERFALLS, AND THEN ... PEACE, THE ILDYLLIC BELL OF THE LEADING RAM AND THE GENTLE FLOCK OF SHEEP ON THE SPACIOUS FIELD. THIS IS BOSNIA, THE COUNTRY OF CURIOUS CONTRASTS.

TRESKAVICA (2088 METRES). IN SOME PLACES LARGE MEADOWS AND PASTURES CAN BE FOUND VERY NEAR THE PEAKS OF THE MOUNTAIN WHICH ARE ABANDONED BY SHEEP ONLY WHEN THE SNOW DRIVES THEM AWAY. THE STINGY SOIL AT THE FOOT OF THE MOUNTAIN MAKES THE POPULATION IN THIS AREA GROW POTATOES AND OTHER VEGETABLES WHICH CAN STAND THE CLIMATE HIGH ABOVE SEA LEVEL.

JAJCE. AN EXTRAORDINARY EXAMPLE OF AN ORIENTAL TOWN; EACH HOUSE WITH ITS OWN VISTA, FRESH AIR AND SUNSHINE. THE WONDERFUL WATERFALLS AT THE FOOT OF THE TOWN HAVE NOT BEEN DEPRIVED OF THIS RIGHT EITHER.

MOSTAR. OLD PART OF THE TOWN. THE UNIQUE TURKISH BRIDGE IN THE SHAPE OF A CRESCENT MAKES EVEN US — LIVING IN AN AGE OF ADVANCED TECHNICAL PROGRESS — ADMIRE THE ARCHITECTS OF THIS BEAUTIFUL AND ELEGANT STRUCTURE.

MODERN TECHNICAL PROGRESS MAKES MAN'S BEST AND OLDEST FRIEND, WHICH PLOUGHED, PULLED, AND CARRIED INSTEAD OF HIM-SELF — THE HORSE — UNNECESSARY. A SPECIAL RACE OF SMALL MOUNTAIN HORSES HAVE BEEN BRED IN BOSNIA — THEY HAVE SLIM LEGS AND ARE VERY NIMBLE, THUS ABLE TO CLIMB STEEP SLOPES EVEN WITHOUT ANY PATHS.

ANOTHER CONTRAST TO THE HARSH BARRENNESS OF STONE FIELDS: GENTLE SLOPES AND SHAPES AT THE FOOT OF WOODED HILLS.

HERE RAINS WERE WASHING THESE MOUNTAINS IN VAIN. THERE IS TOO LITTLE EARTH FOR SO MUCH STONE... EVEN GRASS AND WEEDS CAN HARDLY GROW HERE.

RAINS AND WINDS HAVE DRIVEN AWAY EVEN THE LAST CRUMB OF EARTH, TAKING IT DOWN TO THE VALLEY. MAN CULTIVATED THE BETTER PARTS OF IT AND PLANTED CONIFER TREE FORESTS IN OTHER PLACES.

THE BANJA LUKA — JAJCE ROAD. THE MODERN WAY OF LIFE IMPOSES ON MAN FAST TRAVELLING AND THIS LEADS TO NEW DANGERS, TO PERPETUAL VIGILANCE AND TENSION OF MAN'S NERVOUS SYSTEM. WILL THIS RESTLESS MAN OF OUR TIMES RUSH ALONG THE WHITE ROAD THROUGH THE BLACK TUNNEL WITHOUT NOTICING ANYTHING BUT THE DARKNESS, OR WILL HE STOP, SIT ON A STONE AND QUIETLY WATCH HOW THE WATER FLOWS BY. ARE THESE BOSNIAN PEASANTS, WALKING SLOWLY, AN ANACHRONISM OR A WARNING?

POČITELJ. THE RESTLESS NERETVA SLOWLY CALMS DOWN IN ITS LOWER COURSE AS IF TRYING TO ENJOY THE BEAUTIES OF THIS PICTURESQUE LANDSCAPE, GREET THE RUINS OF THE MEDIEVAL TOWN, HIGH UP ON THE ROCK, AS WELL AS THE INTERESTING TURKISH BUILDINGS DATING FROM THE 15th AND 16th CENTURIES.

THE BOGUMIL NECROPOLIS AT RADIMLJE. THIS IS THE LARGEST AND THE MOST IMPORTANT BOGUMIL CEMETERY. IT CONSISTS OF 133 »STEĆCI« — TOMBSTONES — OF VARIOUS SHAPE AND SIZES. THESE TOMBSTONES ARE DECORATED BY A GREAT VARIETY OF ORNAMENTS, BY RELIEFS OF KNIGHTS, WARRIORS, ANIMALS, AS WELL AS HUNTING AND WAR SCENES. THE POETIC INSCRIPTIONS ON TOMBSTONES REVEAL THE GLOOMY HOPELESSNESS OF THE PEOPLE WHO HAVE BEEN LYING UNDER THESE HEAVY STONES FOR CENTURIES.

CORN AND FORESTS ARE NOT ONLY USEFUL AS THEY PROVIDE FOOD AND FIREWOOD, BUT ALSO TIMBER. IN THE AGE OF PRE-FABRI-
CATED BUILDING ELEMENTS IT IS PERHAPS A LITTLE CURIOUS TO SEE THESE PEASANT HOUSES COVERED BY STRAW AND SHINGLES. YET,
WE MUST NOT FORGET THAT NOT ONE CENTURY HAS PASSED SINCE SUCH ROOFS COULD BE FOUND IN LARGE EUROPEAN TOWNS.

BLIDINJE LAKE (1180 METRES ABOVE SEA LEVEL, WITH A SURFACE OF 3.2 SQUARE KILOMETRES). THE LAKE IS SITUATED AT DUGI BOLJ, BETWEEN ČVRSNICA, MUHARNICA AND VRAN MOUNTAINS, AND BY ITS VERY ACT OF EXISTENCE IT GIVES A NEW AND HIGHER VALUE TO THESE GLOOMY MOUNTAINS.

ANOTHER »STEĆAK« — RELENTLESS WARNING ON THE PASSING CHARACTER OF HUMAN LIFE: "I ALSO USED TO BE AS YOU ARE, BUT YOU WILL ALSO BECOME ME".

THE RAVANICA MONASTERY. THE MONASTERY WAS BUILT BY THE SERBIAN DUKE LAZAR IN 1381, LESS THAN EIGHT YEARS BEFORE THE DISASTROUS BATTLE OF KOSOVO. THE CHURCH IS AN EXAMPLE OF THE MORAVIAN SCHOOL, RICHLY DECORATED BY STONE ORNAMENTS, ITS INTERIOR ABOUNDING IN FRESCOES, AMONG WHICH THE MOST NOTEWORTHY ARE THOSE OF DUKE LAZAR AND DUCHESS MILICA.

PORTAL OF THE MOST BEAUTIFUL AND MOST IMPORTANT SERBIAN CHURCH. THE CHURCH WAS BUILT IN THE FIRST PART OF THE 14th CENTURY. IT IS A SUCCESSFUL BLENDING OF ROMANESQUE, GOTHIC AND BYZANTINE ARCHITECTURE. ITS CAREFULLY BALANCED VOLUME, ITS RICH DECORATIVE ORNAMENTS, ABOUT THIRTY BIFORIA AND TRIFORIA, THE WEALTH OF SCULPTURES AND FRESCOES — SOME OF SAINTS AND OTHERS TAKEN FROM HISTORY — MAKE THIS ONE OF THE MOST IMPORTANT SERBIAN MEDIEVAL MONUMENTS.

TREPČA, A MEDIEVAL MINING VILLAGE WITH A COLONY OF SAXONS AND PEOPLE FROM DUBROVNIK (WHO SETTLED HERE IN 1303), IS TODAY ONE OF THE LARGEST LEAD AND SILVER MINES IN EUROPE. THE GENTLE SURROUNDINGS OF THE MINE, ITS WATERS, FIELDS, AND THE GENTLE SLOPES OF THE HILLS CAN BE TAKEN AS AN INTRODUCTION TO THE PICTURESQUE AND VARIED LANDSCAPE OF SERBIA.

GOLIJA, MOUNTAIN. WHAT WONDERFUL AND GLOOMY SCULPTURES CAN BE SHAPED BY BUSHES, BUT THE FATE OF ONE TREE DOES NOT PREVENT THE WHOLE WOOD FROM GROWING DEFIANTLY. THIS BARREN LAND, DEVASTATED BY FIRE, WILL AGAIN BE COVERED BY DARK GREEN CONIFER TREE FORESTS.

HOMOLJE. BETWEEN THE REED AND THE SKIES THERE IS NOTHING BUT THESE STRANGE, LONELY TREES WHICH WOULD LOOK LONELY EVEN IN A DENSE WOOD.

THE KLADNICA VILLAGE IN SANDŽAK. THIS LITTLE FIELD WOULD STRIKE US QUITE DIFFERENTLY IF THE SCATTERED HOUSES WERE CONCENTRATED IN ONE SETTLEMENT. BUT IT IS JUST THE FACT THAT THEY ARE SCATTERED, AS IF IT WERE AIMLESSLY, THAT MAKES THEM VISUAL ACCENTS IN A SYMPHONY OF NATURE AND HUMAN POWER.

THE BELLS OF THE MANASIJA MONASTERY UNDER THE RUINOUS WALL. THE MONASTERY WAS BUILT AT THE BEGINNING OF THE 15TH CENTURY AND SURROUNDED BY A THICK WALL AND ELEVEN POWERFUL TOWERS. THE FORTRESS LOST ITS STRATEGIC IMPORTANCE A LONG TIME AGO AND IS SLOWLY DILAPIDATING. IN THE CHURCH OF THE MONASTERY A GREAT NUMBER OF WONDERFUL FRESCOES FROM THE 15TH CENTURY HAS EITHER BEEN RUINED OR BADLY DAMAGED.

THE SRETENJE MONASTERY, ONE OF THE EIGHT MONASTERIES BUILT BETWEEN THE 13TH AND 17TH CENTURIES IN THE OVČARSKO-KABLARSKA CRAG. THE RESTLESS WESTERN MORAVA FLOWS THROUGH THE CRAG, MEETIND ON ONE BANK THE STEEP AND BARREN ROCKS, AND ON THE OTHER THE MOUNTAIN COVERED IN DENSE WOODS.

CANYONS OF THE DRINA. PARTLY SILENT AND MURMURING, PARTLY FIERCE AND FOAMING, THE DRINA FLOWS THROUGH AREAS OF FANTASTIC SHAPES AND OPENS ITS BREASTS TO CHEERFUL SWIMMERS, PERSISTANT ANGLERS, DARING RAFTSMEN AND EVEN MORE DARING CANOEISTS.

THE WHITE DRIM. THE STONE HAS VIOLATED THE RULES OF THE GAME: IT REFUSED TO ACCEPT THE GREY PATINA DEFYING WITH ITS WHITENESS ALL ONSLAUGHTS OF OXIGEN AND SUNSHINE.

THE CHURCH OF LAZARICA, AN ENDOWMENT OF DUKE LAZAR (14TH CENTURY), ONE OF THE MOST BEAUTIFUL MONUMENTS OF THE MORAVIAN SCHOOL OF ARCHITECTURE. THE CHURCH IS BUILT IN STONE AND BRICK ALTERNATELY WHICH ACCOUNTS FOR ITS SPECIAL PICTURESQUENESS AND CHARM. THE RICH ARCHITECTURE, THE COLUMNS, PILASTERS, NICHES, WREATHES, ACHITRAVES, WINDOWS LIKE CHESSBOARDS, THE WELL-PROPORTIONED DECORATIONS COMPLEMENT THE BASIC DESIGN AND VOLUME OF THE CHURCH AS CONCEIVED BY THE ARCHITECT.

THE PATRIARCHATE OF PEĆ. THE SERBIAN CHURCH SECEDED IN 1346 FROM THE PATRIARCHATE IN CONSTANTINOPLE WHICH ANATHE-MIZED THE SERBIAN CHURCH AND EMPEROR DUŠAN IN 1352. THE TURKS ABOLISHED THE PATRIARCHATE AT THE BEGINNING OF THE 16TH CENTURY, BUT FOUNDED IT AGAIN UNDER PATRIARCH MACHARIUS, BROTHER OF THE GRAND VIZIER MEHMED SOKOLOVIĆ. IT WAS ABOLISHED AGAIN IN 1766 BECAUSE OF SERBIAN PARTICIPATION IN THE WARS AGAINST TURKS, TO BE RE-ESTABLISHED IN 1920. IN THIS HARSH AND INACCESSIBLE PART OF THE COUNTRY, THIS SPECIMEN OF MEDIEVAL ARCHITECTURE WITH ITS FINE DESIGN, COMPO-SITION AND VOLUME STRIKES THE ONLOOKER VERY POWERFULLY.

THE MIRUŠA RIVER IN KOSMET. THE WATERS TEAR, CARRY AND DESTROY EVERYTHING WITH THEIR UNIQUE PERSEVERANCE. THESE HEAVY AND IMPRESSIVE STONE VAULTS WILL ALSO BE CARRIED AWAY BY THE ALL-DESTRUCTIVE POWER OF WHITE FOAM.

KOSOVRAŠKA IN THE RADIVA VALLEY. THESE ARE NOT FROZEN WATERFALLS, BUT FANTASTIC SULPHUR STALACTITES FLOWING PROTECTIVELY OVER THE HUGE STONE BARRIERS.

THE MEDIEVAL MONASTERY OF GORNJAK, BUILT IN 1380, BURNT DOWN BY TURKS IN 1788, RESTORED IN THE 19TH CENTURY. LIKE MOST MEDIEVAL FORTRESSES AND MONASTERIES IT WAS BUILT IN AN INACCESSIBLE CRAG, PARTLY EVEN DUG INTO THE CRAG ITSELF. THE GORNJAČKA CRAG IS IN ITS RAW WILDERNESS AND STEEPNESS ONE OF THE MOST IMPRESSIVE GORGES IN SERBIA. THE MLAVA FLOWS THROUGH THE CRAG.

DETAIL FROM THE STUDENICA MONASTERY. THIS MONASTERY, TOO, WAS BUILT IN AN INACCESSIBLE PART OF THE COUNTRY, IN THE STUDENICA RIVER CANYON. THERE ARE THREE CHURCHES ON THE MONASTERY GROUNDS, BUILT BETWEEN THE 12TH AND THE 14TH CENTURIES. THE MOST IMPORTANT OF THESE IS THE CHURCH OF OUR LADY, WHOSE VALUE DOES NOT ONLY LIE IN THE CAREFULLY BALANCED VOLUME AND SOME OF THE MOST BEAUTIFUL DECORATIONS OF THE 12TH CENTURY IN THIS COUNTRY, BUT ALSO IN THE RICH FRESCOES FROM THE BEGINNING OF THE 13TH CENTURY. IN ST. NICHOLAS CHURCH THERE ARE WONDERFUL FRESCOES FROM THE BEGINNING OF THE 14TH CENTURY. STUDENICA IS ONE OF THE FEW MONASTERIES WHERE — IN ADDITION TO ARCHITECTURE AND PAINTINGS — A RICH TREASURY OF SACRAL OBJECTS AND PRECIOUS MANUSCRIPTS HAVE BEEN PRESERVED, AMONG OTHERS NEMA-NJA'S BIOGRAPHY, THE MOST BEAUTIFUL WORK OF MEDIEVAL SERBIAN LITERATURE.

ŠUMADIJA. AFTER MOUNTAIN GORGES, VERTICAL ROCKS, RUGGED AND INACCESSIBLE MOUNTAIN RIDGES, ROCKS AND VALLEYS, AFTER ALL THESE HARD LANDSCAPES OF SERBIA, HERE WE ARE AMONG GENTLE AND PLAYFUL HILLS OF ŠUMADIJA, OF HARMONIOUS SHAPES AND WELL-BALANCED COLOURS OF THE SOIL AND VEGETATION.

TITOVO UŽICE. SITUATED IN A WONDERFUL FERTILE VALLEY IT WAS INHABITED EVEN IN PRE-HISTORICAL TIMES. SEVERAL TIMES IN THE COURSE OF ITS HISTORY UŽICE PLAYED AN IMPORTANT PART, THE MOST INPORTANT, HOWEVER, BEING THAT PLAYED IN LAST WAR. AS EARLY AS IN AUTUMN 1941 BODIES OF THE NEW PEOPLE'S GOVERNMENT WERE FORMED HERE, AND IN UŽICE ITSELF THE HEADQUARTERS OF THE PEOPLE'S LIBERATION COMMITTEE HAD ITS SEAT. THE GERMANS ATTACKED THE TOWN WITH POWERFUL FOR CES AND CONQUERED IT AFTER HARD AND BLOODY BATTLES INWHICH WHOLE BATTALIONS WERE KILLED.

KLADOVO IN THE DJERDAP GORGE ON THE DANUBE. THE TOWN WAS FOUNDED BY SULEIMAN THE MAGNIFICENT IN 1542, USING IT AS A SPRINGBOARD FOR HIS ATTACKS ON RUMANIAN STRONGHOLDS ON THE OTHER BANK OF THE DANUBE. IN THE 18TH CENTURY FIERCE BATTLES WERE FOUGHT HERE BETWEEN THE TURKISH AND AUSTRIAN ARMIES. THE TOWN WAS DESTROYED AND LATER RESTORED. SOME OF THE REMAINS HAVE BEEN WELL PRESERVED, ABOVE ALL THE ENTRANCE PART AND THE DEFENCE TOWER. NOT FAR FROM THIS PLACE VALUABLE REMAINS FROM ROMAN TIMES HAVE BEEN FOUND.

A SEA OF WHEAT-FIELDS. THE FERTILE UKRAINIAN EARTH COVERS THIS LARGE DANUBIAN PLAIN, CALLED IN PAST CENTURIES »THE GRANARY OF EUROPE«.

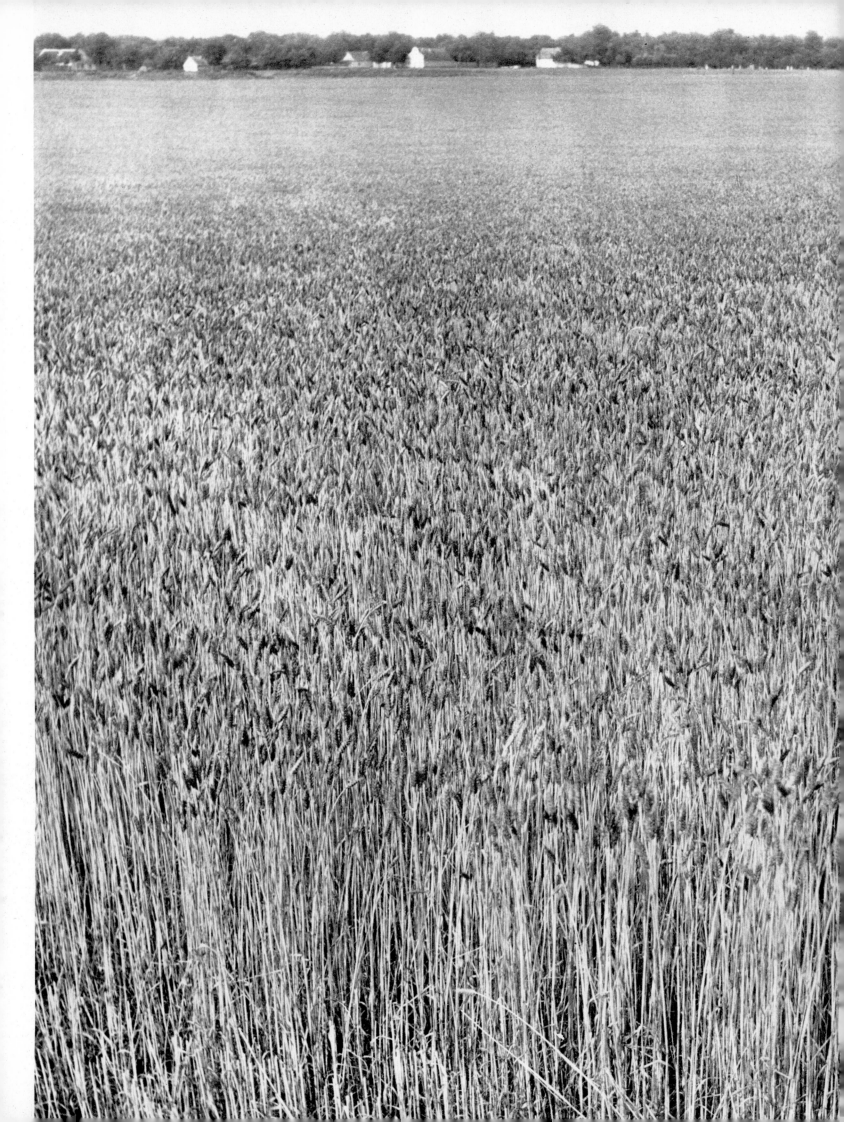

PRIZREN. AT THE PICTURESQUE FOOT OF ŠAR-PLANINA THE TOWN IS SITUATED CALLED BY ROMANS THERANDA. IN THE MIDDLE OF THE 15TH CENTURY PRIZREN WAS CONQUERED BY TURKS WHO GAVE IT ITS ORIENTAL FEATURES WHICH IT HAS RETAINED UP TO THE PRESENT DAY. HERE WE FIND NUMEROUS CULTURAL AND HISTORIC SIGHTS: THE OLD FORTRESS, ST. SPAS' CHURCH FROM THE 14TH CENTURY, SINAN PASHA'S MOSQUE, ONE OF THE MOST MONUMENTAL MOSQUES IN THE COUNTRY, DECORATED BY MARBLE WHICH THE TURKS TOOK FROM ST. ARCHANGEL'S CHURCH, EMPEROR DUŠAN'S MAIN ENDOWMENT.

THE TERZIJSKI BRIDGE IN KOSMET. THE LIVELY TRAFFIC WITH THE EAST IN THE TIMES OF TURKISH RULE (BETWEEN THE 15TH AND 19TH CENTURIES) MADE GOOD ROADS AND FIRM BRIDGES INDISPENSABLE. THIS IS ONE OF THE NUMEROUS STONE BRIDGES, IMPRESSING THE VISITOR BY THEIR BEAUTY AND STURDY STRUCTURE. ALL OF THESE BRIDGES ARE STILL IN USE FOR THE MODERN FAST TRAFFIC.

DRYING HEMP AT VRANJSKA SPA. SERBIA ABOUNDS IN THERMAL SPRINGS WHICH ATTRACT NUMEROUS YUGOSLAV AND FOREIGN TOURISTS WITH THEIR MEDICINAL WATERS, WONDERFUL LANDSCAPES AND RICH FOLKLORE.

SPRING OF THE MLAVA. A ROMANTIC LANDSCAPE IN EASTERN SERBIA: UNTROUBLED HARMONY BETWEEN HILLS AND MEADOWS, WOOD AND WATER, THE PEACE WHICH IS BADLY NEEDED BY MODERN MAN EXPOSED TO THE ROARING NOISES OF MACHINES AND THE RUSHING MOTOR CARS.

THE HIGHWAY CUTTING THROUGH YUGOSLAVIA FROM HER NORTHEASTERN TO THE SOUTHEASTERN BORDER TOUCHES ALL TOWNS OF
ANY IMPORTANCE AND PASSES THROUGH VARIOUS LANDSCAPES: SOMETIMES IT PIERCES THROUGH RUGGED MOUNTAINS AND SOMETIMES
IT FINDS ITS WAY THROUGH GENTLE HILLS, SOMETIMES IT CROSSES ENDLESS PLAINS AND SOMETIMES IT FOLLOWS THE DROWSY
FLOW OF RIVERS.... AS HERE, FOR EXAMPLE, IN THE BEAUTIFUL AND SPACIOUS MORAVA RIVER VALLEY.

THE OLD TOWN OF SMEDEREVO, ON THE RIGHT BANK OF THE DANUBE, WAS ERECTED BY THE DESPOT DJURADJ BRANKOVIĆ IN 1430. THE STURDY WALLS, FORTIFIED BY 25 POWERFUL TOWERS, WERE AN IMPREGNABLE FORTIFICATION WHICH COULD BE CONQUERED ONLY THROUGH TREASON AS IT HAPPENED IN 1459. UNTIL THE LAST WAR THE TOWN WAS WELL PRESERVED. THE EXPLOSION OF AMMUNITION IN 1941 AND THE AIR RAID IN 1944 CAUSED GREAT DAMAGE, BUT EVEN THE GHASTLY RUINS CAN CONVEY THE PICTURE OF ONE OF THE MOST POWERFUL MEDIEVAL FORTIFICATIONS IN EUROPE.

ABOVE THE CHILLY BOHINJ LAKE RISES KOMNA WITH ITS WONDERFUL SKI GROUNDS. WE CAN SEE TRACES OF ONLY ONE ANIMAL ON THE FRESH SNOW, WHILE FIVE SKIERS MOVE ALONG THEIR OWN PATH... AND THIS REVEALS EVERYTHING.

THE JULIAN ALPS. THE CONIFER TREE WOODS UNDER THE BARE AND CONSTANTLY FROZEN PEAKS WHICH HAUGHTILY CHALLENGE ALPINISTS TO A NOT SO NAïVE AND HARMLESS DUEL. ALPINE LANDSCAPES ARE HERE AS MAGNIFICENT AND BEAUTIFUL AS IN SWITZER-LAND AND AUSTRIA.

THE SILVER
SOČA RUNS
THROUGH THE
VALLEYS OF
THE JULIAN
ALPS, ALONG-
SIDE IT RUNS
THE WHITE
ROAD WHICH
OPENS NEW
VISTAS AND
UNEXPECTED
LANDSCAPES
AT EVERY
STEP.

THE ŠKOCJAN-
SKA CAVE,
NOT FAR
FROM DIVAČA
APERT FROM
POSTOJNA.
THIS IS ONE
OF THE MOST
ATTRACTIVE
CAVES IN
EUROPE. THE
SUBTERRA-
NEAN COURSE
OF THE RIVER
WITH ITS
LAKES AND
WATERFALLS
GIVES THIS
RESTLESS UN-
DERGROUND
CAVE AN
UNUSUAL
CHARM.

THE POSTOJNA CAVES. ONE OF THE MOST BEAUTIFUL AND LARGEST CAVES IN THE WORLD. THE OVERALL LENGTH OF THESE PASSAG-
ES AMOUNTS TO 19 KILOMETRES. THROUGH THE CAVE FLOWS THE PIVKA WHICH RUNS BOTH ON THE SURFACE AND UNDERGROUND.
THE CAVE WAS KNOWN IN THE 18TH CENTURY. TODAY IT IS ILLUMINATED BY ELECTRIC LIGHTS AND A LITTLE ELECTRIC TRAIN TAKES
VISITORS TO ITS MYSTERIOUS DEPTHS, INTERWOVEN WITH AN AMAZING NETWORK OF STALACTITES AND STALAGMITES IN CORRI-
DORS AND SPACIOUS HALLS, SOMETIMES OVER 50 METRES HIGH.

THE BOVA WATERFALLS. WOODS, ROCKS AND WATER, UNDERGROUND AND ABOVE GROUND CHASMS AND RAVINES — STRESSED NOTES
IN THE LIVELY HARMONY OF THE SLOVENE LANDSCAPE.

THE OLD TOWN OF LJUBLJANA. ON THE STEEP AND WOODED HILL ABOVE ANCIENT EMONA A FORTIFIED TOWN WAS ERECTED IN THE SLAVIC AGE (PROBABLY IN THE 9TH CENTURY), EVIDENTLY ON REMAINS OF ILLYRIAN, CELTIC AND ROMAN FORTIFICATIONS. ITS PRESENT APPEARANCE DATES FROM THE 15TH AND 16TH CENTURIES, WHEREAS THE CLOCKTOWER WAS BUILT IN THE 19TH CENTURY.

LJUBLJANA. THIS RENAISSANCE MONASTERY WITHIN THE COMPLEX OF KRIŽANKA — WHERE ONCE STOOD THE CHURCH OF THE GER-
MAN ORDER OF CRUSADERS — WAS RESTORED BY THE SLOVENE ARCHITECT PLEČNIK — WHO WAS ALSO ENGAGED AT THE RESTO-
RATION OF THE HRADČANI CASTLE IN PRAGUE.

PREDJAMSKI GRAD. IN A CAVE ON A CLIFF 123 METRES HIGH, THE UNIQUELY FORTIFIED RETREAT OF ERASMO PREDJAMSKI (15th CENTURY) WAS BUILT AGAIN TOWARDS THE END OF THE 16th CENTURY. TODAY IN THIS IMPREGNABLE FORTIFICATION ARCHEOLOGICAL REMAINS OF GREAT VALUE FROM THIS AREA LIE INSTEAD OF GUNS AND GUNPOWDER.

OTOČEC ON THE KRKA. ONE OF THE NUMEROUS SLOVENE FORTIFIED MEDIEVAL CASTLES. IT HAS BEEN RENOVATED AND TURNED INTO A EXCURSION SPOT ALONGSIDE THE ZAGREB-LJUBLJANA HIGHWAY.

LAKE BOHINJ. IN A MOUNTAIN VALLEY, SQUEEZED BETWEEN THE MASSIVE JULIAN ALPS, STRETCHES THE LARGEST LAKE IN SLOVE-NIA. THE SPACIOUS GREEN VALLEY, THE DARK BLUE WATER OF THE LAKE, AND THE AWE-INSPIRING STEEP MOUNTAIN SPURS MAKE MAN FIND HIS DIVIDED SELF IN THIS CLASH BETWEEN THE ROUGH AND THE GENTLE.

LAKE BLED. IN A WONDERFUL VALLEY, ENCLOSED BY THE JULIAN ALPS AND THE KARAVANKAS, WE FIND THE MOST BEAUTIFUL LAKE IN SLOVENIA. THE LUSCIOUS CONIFEROUS FORESTS, THE OLD CASTLE OF BLED, THE UP-TO-DATE HOTELS AND VILLAS MAKE THIS LAKE THE MOST IMPORTANT RESORT IN CONTINENTAL YUGOSLAVIA. SKATING AND WALKING ARE OF PARTICULAR INTEREST, AND SO IS ALSO DRIVING CARS ON THE FROZEN LAKE.

COVERED BY A SNOW CAP, KRVAVEC (1853 METRES) PEACEFULLY WATCHES HOW THE CLOUDS DROWN THE FOREST, CREATING AN IMMEASURABLE WHITE SEA.

THE VRŠIĆ PASS (1611 METRES). THIS IS ONE OF THE MOST BEAUTIFUL AND THE HIGHEST SADDLE-BACKS IN EUROPE. THE VIEW FROM THE PASS OVER THE ALPINE PEAKS, THE FERTILE TRENTA VALLEY AND THE SPRING OF THE SOČA IS SUPERB.

POKLJUKA. NOT FAR FROM BLED WE FIND THIS WINTER SPORTS CENTRE WHERE NATIONAL AND INTERNATIONAL CONTESTS ARE HELD IN ALL CLASSICAL WINTER SPORTS EVENTS. BARE AND ROUGH ALPINE PEAKS ARE HERE TRANSFORMED INTO GENTLE HILLS COVERED IN DENSE AND FRAGRANT CONIFER TREE WODS.

LOGARSKA DOLINA. ONE OF THE MOST BEAUTIFUL PARTS OF SLOVENIA. THIS VALLEY WAS CREATED BY MELTING GLACIERS. IT IS SEVEN KILOMETRES LONG. ABOVE THE FLOWERY MEADOWS AND THE RICH VEGETATION RISES A WHOLE CHAIN OF MOUNTAINS, EACH OF WHICH IS OVER TWO THOUSAND METRES HIGH. AT THE BOTTOM OF THE VALLEY THERE IS THE SPRING OF THE SAVINJA WITH THE WATERFALL (LOGARSKI ŠUM) WHICH IS 120 METRES HIGH.

THE DWARFED AND WITHERED BRANCHES OF TREES, LIKE BRAVE OUTPOSTS SEEM TO BE SAYING THAT THE REALM OF STONE PEAKS IS FOR THEM IMPREGNABLE.

THE FIR-TREE SPRINGING UP FROM ROCKS SEEMS TO SEND US THE LAST GREETINGS OF THE MAGNIFICENT AND INTIMIDATING, BUT STILL ALLURING SLOVENE MOUNTAINS WHICH IRRESISTIBLY ATTRACT US OFFERING US A SHARE IN THE POWER AND BEAUTY.

ONE OF THE COUNTLESS WATERFALLS OF THE KORANA WHICH FORM A UNIQUE EUROPEAN WONDER: THE SIXTEEN PLITVICE LAKES, SURROUNDED BY ROCKS AND TRAVERTINE BARRIERS, AND SMOTHERED WITH RICH VEGETATION.

THE PLITVICE LAKES — A SYMPHONY OF ROCKS, GREEN VEGETATION, AND THE ROARING IRRIDISCENT AND WHITE FOAM. COLOURS ARE CHANGING HERE BECAUSE THE HARD BASE UNDERNEATH IS NOT DEAD BUT ALIVE, IT DOES NOT SHRINK BUT GROWS. THIS IS A KIND OF STONE THAT THE WATER DOES NOT DESTROY BUT MAKES IT GROW. RESTLESS MICRO-ORGANISMS CONSTANTLY DEPOSIT LIME-STONE; AND WHERE MOST OF THE WATER FALLS THE HUGE BARRIERS GROW EVEN QUICKER.

ŠESTINE. THE PICTURESQUE SURROUNDINGS OF ZAGREB — OF THIS GREEN TOWN SCATTERED ON COUNTLESS WOODED SPURS OF MEDVED-
NICA AND THE GREEN SAVA VALLEY — INSPIRED MANY A CROAT POET AND REFRESHED THE CITIZENS OF THE TOWN BY THEIR
GREAT CHARM.

VARAŽDIN. UNTIL THE SECOND HALF OF THE 16th CENTURY VARAŽDIN WAS THE CAPITAL OF CROATIA. EVEN LATER, UNTIL 1776, THE CROATIAN BAN AND PARLIAMENT HAD THEIR SEAT IN THIS TOWN. IN THE PICTURE: THE OLD FORTRESS OF VARAŽDIN, A MEDIEVAL FORTIFICATION, WHICH ACQUIRED ITS PRESENT APPEARANCE IN THE 16th CENTURY. THIS IS ONE OF THE MOST BEAUTIFUL AND THE BEST PRESERVED FORTIFICATIONS IN NORTHERN CROATIA.

VELIKI TABOR, THE MOST MONUMENTAL AND BEST PRESERVED MEDIEVAL FORTIFICATION IN CROATIA. STURDY WALLS, DEFENCE TOWERS, SEMI-CIRCULAR BASTIONS ON CONSOLES, THE RENAISSANCE COURTYARD AND RENAISSANCE ADDITION TO THE GOTHIC STRUCTURE OF THE MAIN TOWER . . . ALL OF IT CAREFULLY BALANCED AND MERGED INTO ONE WHOLE, INTO A RARE PEARL OF MEDIEVAL ARCHITECTURE.

GENTLE GLADES PENSIVELY SLOPE INTO THE VALLEY AND INVISIBLY SEEM TO PUSH THE TREES OF THE RICH FOREST DOWN TO HIDE THE CALM FLOW OF THE RIVER. BUT MAN WANTED THE RIVER FOR HIMSELF, HE PUT ACROSS IT STURDY CONCRETE AND STONE BEAMS, WHILE HE PUSHED AWAY THE FOREST PLOUGHING HIS FIELDS.

THIS SEEMINGLY MOTIONLESS MIRROR IS CONSTANTLY MOVING, PEACEFULLY AND NOISELESSLY, AS COUNTRY LIFE FREED FROM THE
TYRANNY OF THE MECHANICAL AGE.

"THE LOVELY GREEN HILLS . . ." BOTH GREEN AND BLUE, YELLOW AND REDDISH, OCRE AND BROWN, THOUSANDS OF COLOURS IN THOUSANDS OF SHAPES, ACCOUNTING FOR THE WONDERFUL BEAUTY OF CROATIAN ZAGORJE, THE HARMONY UNTOUCHED BY ANYTHING FALSE AND EXTRANEAOUS, UNTOUCHED BY ANYTHING THAT WOULD NOT BECOME PART OF THE LIVING TISSUE OF THIS LANDSCAPE.

KRKA WATERFALLS. ANOTHER KARST RIVER, ANOTHER RARE EUROPEAN BEAUTY. THIS IS ONLY A DETAIL OF ITS NUMEROUS WATER-FALLS, OF THE RIVER THAT IS KNOWN TO BE THE RICHEST IN TRAVERTINE IN EUROPE. LIKE ON THE PLITVICE LAKES THESE BARRIERS ARE STEADILY GROWING, THUS CAUSING EVER LARGER MASSES OF WATER FLOW OVER THEM.

AUTUMN HAS REACHED THE PLITVICE LAKES TOO. FLOWERS HAVE WITHERED, LEAVES HAVE FALLEN, THERE IS NOTHING BUT THE NAKED BEAUTY OF STONE AND WATER.

BELEC. THE BEAUTIFUL DETAIL OF THE ALTAR IS ONLY A DISCREET OVERTURE TO THE SYMPHONY OF MARIJA SNJEŽNA CHURCH, OF THIS MOST BEAUTIFUL MONUMENT OF CROATIAN BAROQUE.

THE ZAGORJE HIGHWAY MEANDERS THROUGH THE PLAYFUL HILLS OF THE CROATIAN ZAGORJE AND TAKES US TO AREAS ABOUNDING IN NATURAL BEAUTY, REMAINS OF MEDIEVAL TOWERS AND FORTRESSES, TO WELL PRESERVED CASTLES AND MANORS FROM PAST CENTURIES.

THE TRAKOŠĆAN CASTLE. THE CASTLE WAS MENTIONED AS EARLY AS THE 14th CENTURY. IT WAS RENOVATED IN THE "NORMAN" STYLE IN THE MIDDLE OF THE 19th CENTURY, AFTER THE EXAMPLE OF RENOVATED CASTLES ON THE RHINE, IN A STYLE THAT NEVER EXISTED IN ORIGINALS. THE CHARM OF THE CASTLE DOES NOT LIE SO MUCH IN ITS ARCHITECTURE, BUT IN ITS SURROUNDINGS, WHICH ARE AMONG THE MOST ROMANTIC IN THE COUNTRY: THE LARGE LAKE WITH WATER-LILIES, THE STREAMS, HILLS, FORESTS ABOUNDING IN GAME, THE UNIQUE PEACE WHICH SPREADS IN ALL DIRECTIONS.

THE WHITE ISLAND LIKE A SEA MONSTER (ABOVE), LIKE AN AIRY WHIRL FORMING A CHEST (BELOW), AND A ROCKY DESERT DIVIDED BY A SENSELESS STONE WALL (RIGHT) ARE ONLY DETAILS OF THE KORNATI. THIS BARREN AND UNINHABITED GROUP OF 125 ISLANDS AND ISLETS, MADE UP OF BULKY LIME-STONE, WITH ITS DESOLATE ROCKY AREAS, FANTASTIC SHAPES, AND RHYTHMIC COMPOSITION PROJECTING FROM THE DEEP AND CLEAR SEA OF THE CENTRAL ADRIATIC, THE KORNATI ARE LIKE SOME ADVENTURE WHICH ONE RARELY EXPERIENCES AND NEVER FORGETS.

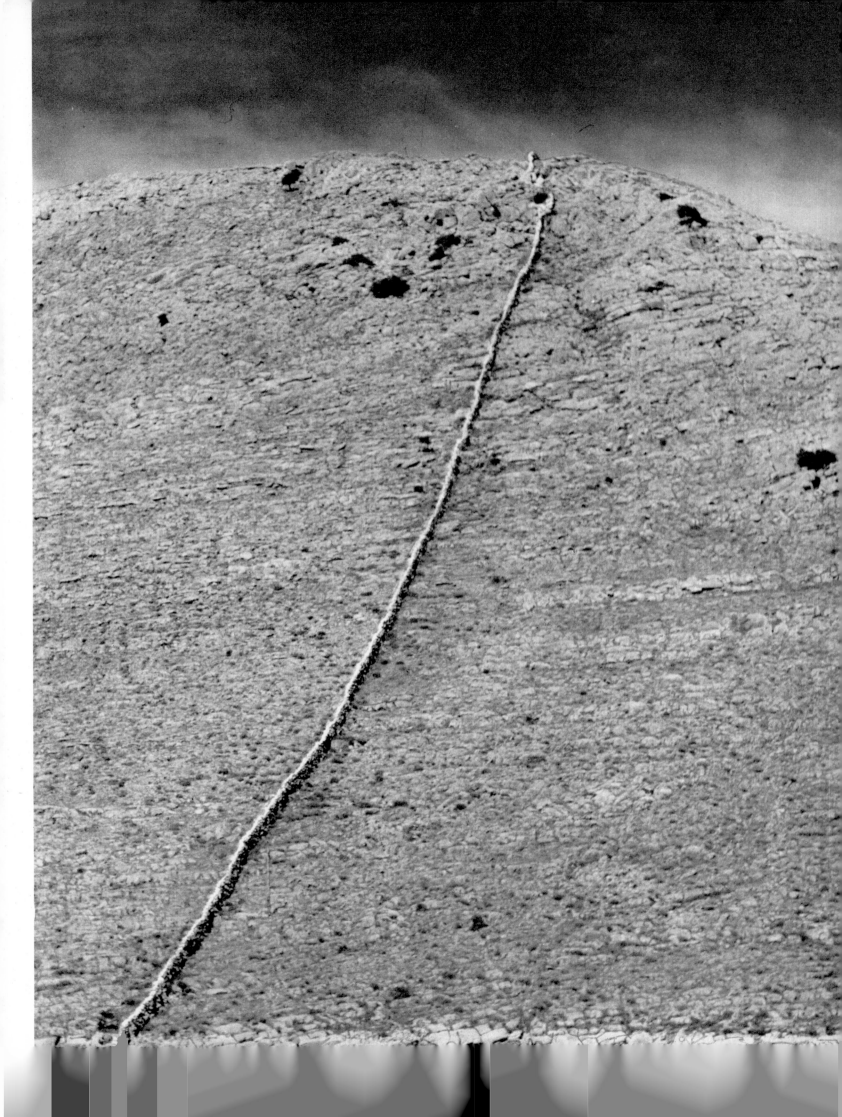

GREEN GRASS AT THE BOTTOM OF THE CETINA RIVER CANYON. PART OF THE DRAIN OF THE UNDERGROUND HYDROELECTRIC PLANT, ONE OF THE LARGEST IN EUROPE, CAN ALSO BE SEEN IN THE PICTURE.

MALI LOŠINJ ON THE ISLAND OF LOŠINJ. THE MEDITERRANEAN CLIMATE AND VEGETATION, THE INDENTED COASTLINE, THE FRESH AND CLEAR INSULAR AIR HELPED TO MAKE THIS A HEALTH RESORT AS EARLY AS THE 19th CENTURY.

VIEW OF THE SPACIOUS SPLIT HARBOUR. IN AND AROUND THE DIOCLETIAN PALACE — THE LARGEST AND THE BEST PRESERVED ANCIENT PALACE IN THE WORLD — SPLIT HAS BEEN DEVELOPING FOR MORE THAN 1,500 YEARS. THIS IS THE BEST KNOWN RESORT IN DALMATIA. THE WEALTH AND VARIETY OF SIGHTS, THE BEAUTIFUL SAND AND GRAVEL BEACHES, THERMAL SPRINGS, UP-TO-DATE TOURIST FACILITIES — ONE OF WHICH CAN BE SEEN IN THIS PICTURE — FAST TRAIN, BUS, PLANE, AND BOAT CONNECTIONS WITH ALL PARTS OF YUGOSLAVIA AND ABROAD ACCOUNT FOR THE FACT THAT VAST NUMBERS OF TOURISTS FROM ALL PARTS OF EUROPE COME TO SPLIT EVERY YEAR.

OMIŠ. STUBBORNLY STRUGGLING ITS WAY THROUGH THE KARST ROCKS THE CETINA FINALLY REACHES ITS POINT OF PEACE. ON ITS ESTUARY, LEANING ON THE CANYON OF THE CETINA, WE FIND THE LITTLE TOWN OF OMIŠ. THE TOWN EXISTED IN PRE-ROMAN TIMES, IN THE MIDDLE AGES IT WAS A RETREAT OF PIRATES, AND TODAY IT IS A FAVOURITE RESORT, LINKED WITH THE ADRIATIC HIGH-WAY BY MEANS OF AN ELEGANT SWINGING BRIDGE.

RAB. THE SMALL TOWN ON THE ISLAND WITH A RICH CULTURAL AND HISTORICAL LEGACY, ABOVE ALL FROM THE MIDDLE AGES.
TREASURY OF CROATIAN ROMANESQUE CULTURE AND ONE OF THE MOST BEAUTIFUL RESORTS IN NORTHERN ADRIATIC.

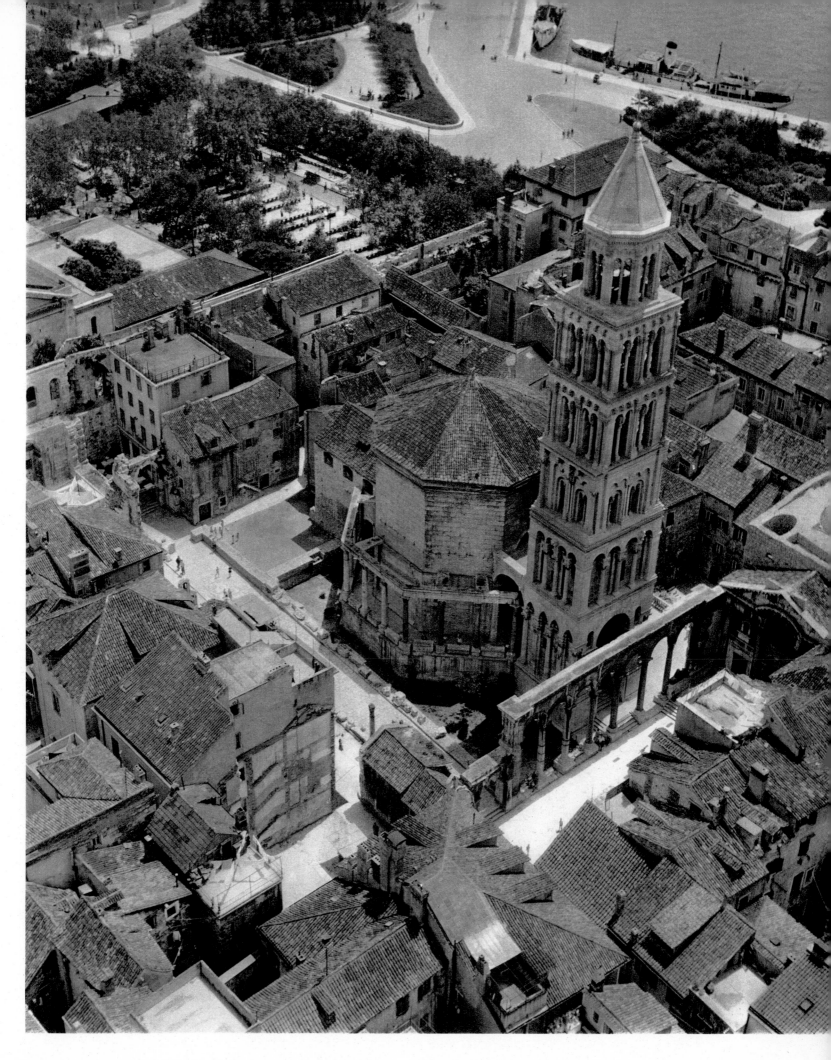

SPLIT. THE HEART OF THE DIOCLETIAN PALACE — ONCE THE EMPEROR'S MAUSOLEUM (TODAY THE CATHEDRAL), HAS PRESERVED
ITS ORIGINAL FORM ALMOST WITHOUT ANY CHANGE. THE ROMANESQUE STEEPLE OF ST. DUJE IS PROUDLY TOWERING OVER THE GREY
ROOFS OF HOUSES BUILT IN PAST CENTURIES.

TROGIR. VIEW FROM THE VESTIBULE OF THE CATHEDRAL AND THE OLD CLOCK-TOWER.

THE COLUMNS OF THE VESTIBULE AND STEEPLE OF EUPHRASIUS' BASILICA IN POREČ. THIS CHURCH WAS BUILT IN THE MIDDLE OF THE 6th CENTURY AND REPRESENTS ONE OF THE MOST BEAUTIFUL AND BEST PRESERVED BASILICAS IN THE WORLD. THE WONDERFUL MOSAICS IN ITS INTERIOR ARE NOT INFERIOR TO THE FAMOUS ONES IN RAVENNA.

PULA. THE AMPHITHEATRE, BUILT UNDER EMPEROR AUGUSTUS, REPRESENTS ONE OF THE BEST PRESERVED ROMAN BUILDINGS IN THE WORLD. OF AN ELLIPTICAL SHAPE (67.5 AND 41.5 METRES), 30 METRES HIGH, IT HAS 72 ARCADES IN ITS STOREYS. THERE USED TO BE 40 ROWS WITH SEATS FOR 23,000 SPECTATORS.

ON THE RIGHT:
THE TOWN-GATE IN ZADAR, ONE OF THE NUMEROUS DALMATIAN TOWNS WHOSE EXISTENCE HAS BEEN UNINTERRUPTED SINCE ILLYRIAN AND ROMAN TIMES.

DUBROVNIK. A STONY PEARL OF THE MEDITERRANEAN. ON A 45 METRES HIGH CLIFF THE POWERFUL WALLS OF THE LOVRIJENAC FOR-
TRESS CAN BE SEEN, WHICH WAS STARTED IN THE 11th AND FINISHED IN 15th CENTURY, THEN ACQUIRING ITS PRESENT APPEARANCE.

ON THE RIGHT:
KLIS: THE DOOR-WAY TO SPLIT AND THE KEY OF THE ADRIATIC, IT WAS ONE OF THE SEATS OF THE CROATIAN NATIONAL RULERS.
THE FORTRESS WAS RAISED ON A HIGH, SPACIOUS, AND FROM ALL SIDES VERTICAL ROCK. SOME PARTS OF THE MEDIEVAL FORTRESS
ARE VERY WELL PRESERVED. WONDERFUL VIEWS OPEN UP FROM ITS TERRACES: FROM ONE SIDE ON THE KARST STONE FIELDS AND
MOUNTAINS, FROM THE OTHER ON THE ROMAN SALONA, SPLIT AND THE ISLANDS IN CENTRAL DALMATIA.

WATER-MELONS ON CRES. IN A STONY SEA A STONY ISLAND, AND ON THE ISLAND A STONY VILLAGE.

PULA. JUPITER'S TEMPLE, BUILT AT THE BEGINNING OF OUR ERA, DURING THE RULE OF EMPEROR AUGUSTUS CESAR. NEXT TO IT STANDS THE TOWN HALL, BUILT IN THE 13th CENTURY IN ROMANESQUE-GOTHIC STYLE. THE PORTAL OF THE BUILDING WAS RENOVATED IN THE 17th CENTURY.

ON THE RIGHT:
SPLIT. MEŠTROVIĆ'S MAGNIFICENT MONUMENT OF THE BISHOP GRGUR NINSKI WHO WAS A PASSIONATE PROMOTER OF GLAGOLITSA SCRIPT AND THE OLD SLAVIC LANGUAGE, UNTIL RECENTLY THE ONLY LANGUAGE NEXT TO LATIN USED IN THE SERVICES OF THE ROMAN CATHOLIC CHURCH.

KORČULA. THE STEEPLE OF THE ROMANESQUE-GOTHIC CATHEDRAL (13th TO 15 th CENTURY), ONE OF THE MOST INTERESTING SACRAL BUILDINGS IN DALMATIA. THE STEEPLE WAS COMPLETED BY THE LOCAL MASTER MARKO ANDRIJIĆ.

VIEW OF THE SOUTH-WESTERN CORNER OF THE DUBROVNIK RAMPARTS AND FORTIFICATIONS (7th TO 15th CENTURY). THE RAMPARTS ARE TWO KILOMETRES LONG, IN SOME PLACES EVEN 22 METRES HIGH AND 5.30 METRES WIDE.

ON THE LEFT:
ST. DONAT'S CHURCH IN ZADAR (BEGINNING OF THE 9th CENTURY) REPRESENTS A MASTER-PIECE OF LATE CROATIAN ARCHITECTURE. ALTHOUGH BUILT OF ROUGHLY DRESSED STONE, ITS CIRCULAR GROUND-PLAN OF THE CAROLINE ROTUNDA, ITS HEIGHT AND STURDINESS MAKE IT LOOK POWERFUL AND MONUMENTAL.

DUBROVNIK. WHILE THE GREATEST PART OF THE COUNTRY THAT IS TODAY YUGOSLAVIA SUFFERED UNDER THE TURKISH YOKE OR FOUGHT ON THE PERMANENTLY BLOODY FRONTIER, DUBROVNIK — THANKS TO ITS POWERFUL RAMPARTS AND EVEN MORE TO ITS SKILFUL DIPLOMACY — ENJOYED THE FREEDOM OF AN INDEPENDENT REPUBLIC, TRADING WITH CHRISTIAN AND MOSLEM COUNTRIES IN THE MEDITERRANEAN, AMASSING GREAT CULTURAL AND MATERIAL WEALTH WITHIN ITS WALLS, UNTIL NAPOLEON BROUGHT AN END TO ITS INDEPENDENCE. TOGETHER WITH FREEDOM WENT THE GOLD, BUT THE CULTURAL AND HISTORIC MONUMENTS HAVE REMAINED IN THE TOWN. TODAY DUBROVNIK IS A UNIQUE SPECIMEN OF ARCHITECTURE AND WITNESS OF ITS SPLENDID PAST.

THE CATHEDRAL IN DUBROVNIK. THIS BEAUTIFUL BAROQUE CATHEDRAL WAS BUILT IMMEDIATELY AFTER THE GREAT EARTHQUAKE IN 1667, ABOVE THE RUINED ROMANESQUE CATHEDRAL, AFTER THE PLANS SUBMITTED BY THE ROMAN ARCHITECT A. BUFFALINI.

ŠIBENIK. THE NORTHERN FRONT OF THIS GOTHIC CATHEDRAL IS ONE OF THE MOST VALUABLE MONUMENTS IN CROATIA. A RICH INTERIOR, HARMONIOUS GOTHIC PORTALS, A FRIEZE OF STONE PORTRAITS BY THE GREAT MASTER JURAJ DALMATINAC, AND PARTICULARLY THE UNIQUE RENAISSANCE ROOF, MAKE THIS CHURCH AN OUTSTANDING EUROPEAN MONUMENT OF ITS KIND.

THE FRANCISCAN MONASTERY IN HVAR. THE WHOLE OF THIS ARCHITECTURAL COMPLEX IS LIKE A PART OF THE SEA AND STONES FROM WHICH IT GREW.

PULA. ANOTHER VIEW OF THE AMPHITHEATRE WHICH IS TELLING EVIDENCE OF THE GREATNESS AND IMPORTANCE OF THIS ANCIENT TOWN. 23,000 SEATS ARE NOT BUILT IN A PROVINCIAL BACKWATER.

ZRMANJA, ANOTHER KARST RIVER, WHICH FROM THIS DESOLATE PLATEAU, SLOWLY BUT STUBBORNLY DECOMPOSED AND WORE AWAY MILLIONS OF TONS OF LIME-STONE, DEPOSITING IT IN THE CALMER VALLEYS AND ON ITS ESTUARY.

LAKE TORAK NEAR DRNIŠ. ONE OF THE COUNTLESS FUNNEL-SHAPED HOLES IN THE LIME-STONE, CAUSED BY SINKING OF THE GROUND.
IF THESE HOLES ARE IMPERMEABLE, AS IN THIS PICTURE, THEN THE WATER COLLECTS FORMING LITTLE KARST LAKES.

GALIČNIK, A VILLAGE ON THE BISTRA MOUNTAIN, 1250 METRES ABOVE SEA LEVEL. THIS IS A WELL-KNOWN MOUNTAIN RESORT ABOVE THE STEEP SLOPES OF THE RADIKA RIVER. FROM THE VILLAGE AND THE HEIGHTS ABOVE IT THERE ARE WONDERFUL VIEWS OF KORAB (2790 m.), KRČIN (2413 m.), STROGOVO (2219 m.), AND OF GREEK AND ALBANIAN MOUNTAINS AND OF RADIKA AND CRNI DRIM RIVER VALLEYS. THE VILLAGE WAS FOUNDED BY THE NOMADIC TRIBE OF SHEPHERDS MIJACI WHICH HAVE PRESERVED THEIR RICH NATIONAL COSTUMES AND EVEN MORE VARIED WEDDING CUSTOMS UP TO THE PRESENT DAY.

ST. NIKOLA ŠIŠEVSKI'S MONASTERY; IN 1308 IT WAS RENOVATED BY KING MILUTIN. SEVERAL VALUABLE FRESCOES ILLUSTRATING JESUS CHRIST'S LIFE, THE WORK BY MIHAJLO AND EUTIHIJA, HAVE BEEN PRESERVED FROM THOSE TIMES.

ON THE WHOLE TERRITORY OF WHAT IS TODAY YUGOSLAVIA THE ROMANS HAVE LEFT A GREAT NUMBER OF MONUMENTS AND BUILDINGS WHICH SPEAK OF THEIR HIGH CIVILISATION. THE REMAINS OF THIS IMPRESSIVE AQUAEDUCT BEAR OUT THE RECORDS OF OLD TRAVELLERS ON THE GREATNESS OF SKUPI (SKOPLJE) — THE CAPITAL OF THE ILLYRIAN TRIBE OF DARDANIANS — WHICH WAS DEVELOPED BY ROMANS INTO A TOWN OF GREAT SPLENDOUR: "IN IT IT IS NOT EASY TO ENUMERATE THE DIVINE TEMPLES, NOR DESCRIBE WITH WORDS THE CASTLES OF ROMAN VETERANS, THE BEAUTY OF SQUARES AND STREETS, FOUNTAINS AND BATHING ESTABLISHMENTS . . ."

KRATOVO, ANOTHER ANCIENT ROMAN SETTLEMENT IN MACEDONIA. HERE THERE WAS A FAMOUS MINE (LEAD, SILVER, GOLD, COPPER, AND IRON) IN THE MIDDLE AGES. SAXONS WERE WORKING IN THIS MINE. THE WHOLE SMALL TOWN IS A UNIQUE CULTURAL AND HISTORIC MONUMENT ON ROMAN, SLAV, AND TURKISH CIVILISATIONS. IN ADDITION TO THE REMAINS OF OLD AND MIDDLE AGES THE MIDDLE CLASS HOUSES FROM THE 19th CENTURY DESERVE SPECIAL MENTION — THEY ARE WONDERFUL SPECIMENS OF MACEDONIAN ARCHITECTURE.

THE FORTRESS OF OHRID, ONE OF THE OLDEST AND LARGEST MEDIEVAL FORTIFICATIONS IN THE COUNTRY. THE ANCIENT FORTRESS WAS RESTORED AND EXPANDED DURING THE REIGN OF EMPEROR SAMUILO WHO MADE A POWERFUL COUNTRY OUT OF THE SMALL MACEDONIAN DUCHY. THE HUGE RAMPARTS, FORTIFIED BY POWERFUL BASTIONS, ENCIRCLE THE MOUNTAIN PEAK AND GO DOWN TO OHRID LAKE. A GREAT NUMBER OF OLD GREEK TOMBSTONE PLAQUES WITH INSCRIPTIONS THAT ARE STILL LEGIBLE WERE USED AS BUILDING MATERIAL. THE FORTRESS WAS OF GREAT STRATEGIC DEFENSIVE IMPORTANCE IN THE LONG PERIOD OF TURKISH RULE.

ST. DIMITRI'S CHURCH (15th CENTURY) AT THE FOOT OF MARKO'S TOWN NEAR PRILEP. THE CHAPEL IS MUCH BETTER PRESERVED THAN THE FORTIFIED TOWN ON THE CLIFF. THE TOWN WAS THE IMPREGNABLE SEAT OF THE LEGENDARY HERO KRALJEVIĆ MARKO, ABOUT WHOM SONGS WERE COMPOSED AND SUNG FOR CENTURIES, SONGS THAT KEPT THE HOPE ALIVE THAT LIBERATION FROM TURKISH SLAVERY MUST COME ONE DAY — BECAUSE MARKO IS STILL ALIVE, HE IS ASLEEP IN A DEEP CAVE, AND PEOPLE SHOULD ONLY PATIENTLY WAIT UNTIL HE WAKES UP.

»NEVESTINSKI ORO« — MACEDONIAN FOLK DANCE TO MARK IMPORTANT OCCASIONS. HOW MUCH SERIOUSNESS AND DIGNITY IN ITS MOVEMENTS, HOW MUCH SILENT SORROW AND HIDDEN EXCITEMENT IN THE FACE OF THE BRIDE, HOW MUCH RESTRAINED PASSION AND HARMONY IN THE RICHLY EMBROIDERED COSTUME, DECORATED BY STRINGS OF DUCATS.

THE NEREZI MONASTERY NEAR SKOPJE. THE MONASTERY WAS BUILT IN 1164 IN THE TYPICAL BYZANTINE STYLE: FIVE CUPOLAS WITH SHALLOW DECORATIONS AND PERFORATED STONE WINDOWS. WELL-PRESERVED FRESCOES FROM THE 12TH CENTURY, HARMONIOUS IN COLOUR AND COMPOSITION, REPRESENT, NEXT TO THEIR INTRINSIC VALUE, THE FIRST ATTEMPTS TO INTRODUCE THE ELEMENT OF REALISM INTO PAINTING WHICH IS BEST MANIFESTED IN THE PAINTING ON THE LAMENTATION OF JESUS CHRIST.

THE GREATEST PART OF THE PELAGONIJA PLAIN — WHICH COMPRISES THE PRILEP VALLEY SURROUNDED BY HIGH MOUNTAINS — IS COVERED BY TOBACCO FIELDS. MACEDONIAN TOBACCO IS ONE OF THE BEST AND MOST APPRECIATED TOBACCOES IN THE WORLD.

ROUND FERTILE PLAINS AND VALLEYS RISE WOOD COVERED MOUNTAINS WITH HIGH PEAKS, GLACIAL LAKES AND LUSCIOUS PASTURES WHERE INNUMERABLE FLOCKS OF SHEEP GRAZE AND WHOSE WOOL IS USED BY THE LOCAL POPULATION FOR THE MANUFACTURE OF THE WELL-KNOWN MACEDONIAN CARPETS.

ST. ĐORĐE'S CHURCH AT STARI NAGORIČIN NEAR KUMANOVO. KING MILUTIN (IN 1313) BUILT THIS CHURCH ON THE RUINS OF THE OLD BYZANTINE CHURCH WHICH PROBABLY DATES FROM THE 11TH CENTURY. THE NEW CHURCH WAS RESTORED IN 1931. A STONE ICONOSTASIS FROM THE BEGINNING OF THE 14TH CENTURY HAS BEEN PRESERVED IN THE INTERIOR OF THE CHURCH. SEVERAL FRESCOES, DATING FROM THE SAME TIME, AND TAKING AN IMPORTANT PLACE IN MEDIEVAL PAINTING, HAVE ALSO BEEN PRESERVED. THE FRESCOES ARE THE WORK OF MIHAILO AND EUTIHIJA WHO DECORATED SEVERAL CHURCHES AND WHO ALSO WORKED AT THE COURT OF KING MILUTIN.

DOJRAN LAKE ON THE FRONTIER BETWEEN YUGOSLAVIA AND GREECE. THE LAKE IS NOT ONLY INTERESTING FOR ITS WONDERFUL MOUNTAINOUS LANDSCAPE, BUT ALSO FOR THE ANCIENT TECHNIQUE OF FISHING WITH THE HELP OF BIRDS, WHICH WERE USED BY OLD DOJRANS, WHO GAVE THE NAME TO THE LAKE.

ARTIFICIAL LAKE OF THE HYDRO-POWER STATION ON THE TRESKA RIVER NEAR SKOPJE. AT THE BOTTOM OF THE ROMANTIC CLIFF THERE IS A SMALL CHAPEL (14TH CENTURY), A VALUABLE SPECIMEN OF MEDIEVAL ARCHITECTURE. THE PECULIAR GROUND-DESIGN, THE CAREFULLY MEASURED ARCHITECTURAL ELEMENTS, AND THE LIVELY DECORATIONS OF RED CERAMICS ADD WARMTH AND GENTLENESS TO THIS STONY WILDERNESS.

STOBI, ANCIENT SETTLEMENT NEAR THE PLACE WHERE THE CRNA REKA FLOWS INTO THE VARDAR. STOBI WAS A TOWN AS EARLY AS THE THIRD CENTURY BEFORE OUR ERA, AND IT WAS AWARDED THE RIGHTS OF A ROMAN COLONY WHICH INCLUDED SELF-GOVERNMENT AND AN INDEPENDENT MINT. IN 479 IT WAS DESTROYED BY EASTERN GOTHS AND IN 518 IT WAS AGAIN COMPLETELY SHATTERED BY AN EARTHQUAKE. BUT THE TOWN DEVELOPED AGAIN ONLY TO BE FINALLY DESTROYED IN THE 14TH CENTURY. IN STOBI WHOLE STREETS HAVE BEEN EXCAVATED, A THEATRE, A TOWN GATE, SEWERAGE, ETC., AND A GREAT NUMBER OF SCULPTURES AND RELIEFS FROM ROMAN TIMES WERE DISCOVERED. FROM THE EARLY CHRISTIAN PERIOD REMAINS OF A BASILICA WERE DISCOVERED TOGETHER WITH TWO CHURCHES, PROBABLY FROM THE 5TH CENTURY. OTHER ITEMS INCLUDE PARTS OF DECORATIONS AND FRAGMENTS OF WONDERFUL MOSAICS WHICH DECORATED THE FLOOR OF THE BASILICA.

ST. JOVAN KANEO. ONE OF THE NUMEROUS MEDIEVAL MONUMENTS ON THE LONG COAST OF OHRID LAKE. THE POLITICAL AND CULTURAL CENTRE OF THE MACEDONIAN STATE WAS FORMED ON THIS COAST OF OHRID LAKE. BETWEEN THE 9TH AND 11TH CENTURY OHRID WAS THE CENTRE OF SLAV CULTURE. KLIMENT AND NAUM, PUPILS OF CYRIL AND METHODIUS, WERE SPREADING LITERACY FROM THIS CENTRE AND LAYING FOUNDATION STONES OF THE LITERATURE OF SOUTHERN SLAVS.

ON THE LEFT: OHRID LAKE (SURFACE: 350 SQUARE KILOMETRES, 286 METRES DEEP, 700 METRES ABOVE SEA LEVEL). NUMEROUS SPRINGS ON THE COAST AND ON THE BOTTOM OF THE LAKE SUPPLY IT WITH FRESH AND CLEAR WATER SO THAT THE BOTTOM OF THE LAKE CAN BE SEEN EVEN WHERE THE WATER IS 22 METRES DEEP. THE MODERATE TEMPERATURE OF THE WATER AND THE AIR, THE LOVELY BEACHES AND BEAUTIFUL LANDSCAPES ATTRACT A STEADILY RISING NUMBER OF TOURISTS. THE LAKE ABOUNDS IN FISH, AND IN THE WORLD OF SCIENCE IT IS KNOWN FOR THE VARIETY OF ITS ALGAE, SMALL CRABS, WORMS AND SNAILS, MANY OF WHICH HAVE DIED OUT IN OTHER PARTS OF THE WORLD.

OHRID, TRPEZICA. THE WONDERFUL COAST OF OHRID LAKE, SOMEWHERE STEEP AND BARREN, IN OTHER PLACES GENTLE AND COVERED IN WOOD, LAVISHLY ENCLOSES THIS LAKE AND ITS WATER WHICH — DEPENDING ON THE WEATHER — CHANGES COLOURS AS A CAPRICIOUS WOMAN HER DRESSES.

FISHING HAS ALWAYS BEEN THE MAIN OCCUPATION OF THE PEOPLE LIVING ON THE COAST OF OHRID. THERE ARE SOME TWENTY KINDS OF FISH IN THE LAKE, THE TROUT FROM OHRID AND OTHER FISH ARE WELL-KNOWN FOR THEIR EXCELLENT MEAT.

THE BRIDE'S NATIONAL COSTUME FROM THE SURROUNDINGS OF TETOVO. THE DIGNIFIED FORM, THE HARMONY OF COLOURS AND MATERIALS, THE RICHLY EMBROIDERED ORNAMENTS, THE ABSENCE OD EMBELLISHMENTS, APART FROM THE STRINGS OF DUCATS IN THE HAIR, THEY ALL SPEAK OF THE REFINED TASTE OF THE MACEDONIAN PEOPLE.

ON THE RIGHT: ST. SOPHIA'S CHURCH AT OHRID (11TH TO 14TH CENTURY). THIS THREE AISLE BASILICA REPRESENTS THE MOST IMPORTANT MONUMENT OF MACEDONIAN MEDIEVAL ARCHITECTURE. THE CHURCH WAS TRANSFORMED INTO A MOSQUE IN THE 16TH CENTURY. IN 1946 IT WAS RESTORED AND THE FRESCOES DISCOVERED AND CLEANED. THE NARROW DOOR OF THE BASILICA IS ONE OF THE NUMEROUS DOORS THAT PRESERVE THE OHRID OF PAST CENTURIES.

KAVADARCI. 2,000 HECTARES OF VINEYARDS COVER THIS FIELD AMONG MOUNTAINS. NEXT TO THE RICH VINEYARDS IS TOBACCO. ON THE FERTILE SOIL OF MACEDONIA TWO PLANTS GROW THAT DO NOT EXIST IN OTHER PARTS OF YUGOSLAVIA: OPIATE AND RICE.

AMONG RUGGED MONTENEGRIN MOUNTAINS THERE ARE CLEARINGS HERE AND THERE, BUT EVEN HERE THE SOIL IS BARREN. AND YET MAN HAS BEEN LIVING HERE FOR CENTURIES. THIS IS ALSO TRUE ABOUT THE MAN WHO LIES UNDER THE OVERTURNED »STEĆAK« AND THE MAN MOVING UNDER HIS ROOF — BOTH OF THEM LED FLOCKS OF SHEEP TO PASTURE, SHEEP THAT WERE ACTUALLY THEIR ONLY PROPERTY.

PERAST, ONCE THE TOWN OF FAMOUS SEA CAPTAINS, SOME OF WHOM COMMANDED NAVIES OF EUROPEAN RULERS. THE DECLINE OF THE TOWN STARTED WHEN STEAMERS TOOK THE PLACE OF THE SAILING SHIP; BUT MANY SACRAL AND OTHER BUILDINGS HAVE BEEN PRESERVED, WITNESSING TO ITS PAST SPLENDOUR. THE TWO ISLETS IN FRONT OF PERAST ARE IMPORTANT CULTURAL AND HISTORIC MONUMENTS. ON THE FIRST WE CAN FIND REMAINS OF A BENEDICTINE ABBEY AND ST. GEORGE'S CHAPEL (FROM THE 12TH CENTURY), AND ON THE SECOND, AN ARTIFICIAL ISLET, WE FIND THE GOSPA OD ŠKRPELJA CHURCH (FROM THE 17TH CENTURY), WITH 68 VALUABLE PAINTINGS.

PLAVSKO LAKE. THE GLITTERING, PEACEFUL MIRROR-LIKE SURFACE OF THIS LAKE SEEMS TO BE REMINDING US OF THE GLACIAL ORIGIN OF THIS LAKE HIGH UP IN THE PROKLETIJE MOUNTAINS. THE GLACIER MELTED A LONG TIME AGO, BUT THE WATER IS STILL FLOWING FROM THE INEXHAUSTIBLE SPRING OF THE ROMANTIC LIM.

DURMITOR (2522 METRES). ONE OF THE HIGHEST AND MOST ROMANTIC MONTENEGRIN MOUNTAINS. BARE STEEP PEAKS, VERTICAL CLIFFS, DEEP CHASMS AND CANYONS, FUNNEL-LIKE HOLES AND CLIFFS, FORESTS, MEADOWS, GLADES, AND SIXTEEN GLACIAL LAKES OF EXTRAORDINARY BEAUTY. IN THE PICTURE: ŽABLJAK, A PICTURESQUE CLIMATIC AND HEALTH RESORT.

NEXT TO SUTOMORE, WITH ONE OF THE MOST BEAUTIFUL BEACHES IN THE ADRIATIC, RISE STEEP MOUNTAIN SPURS. ON THE TOP OF THE MOUNTAIN WE SEE RUINS OF THE MEDIEVAL HAJ-NEHAJ FORTIFICATION WHICH WAS ERECTED BY VENETIANS IN THEIR ATTEMPT TO INSURE SAFE NAVIGATION IN THIS PART OF THE ADRIATIC. THE RAMPARTS WERE FURTHER FORTIFIED BY TURKS FOR THE PROTECTION OF THEIR CARAVANS WHICH WERE ATTACKED BY MONTENEGRINS.

SVETI STEFAN. ONCE A FORTIFIED PIRATE STRONGHOLD, THEN A FISHING VILLAGE, ONLY TO BE TRANSFORMED INTO A TOWN-HOTEL WHOSE EXTERNAL APPEARANCE HAS REMAINED UNTOUCHED BUT WHOSE INTERIOR HAS BEEN ADAPTED IN ACCORDANCE WITH ALL DEMANDS OF MODERN COMFORT.

ULCINJ, THE SOUTHERNMOST TOWN ON THE YUGOSLAV COAST OF THE ADRIATIC. IT WAS FOUNDED BY KOLHIDIANS, TAKEN OVER BY GREEKS AND THEN BY ROMANS. IN THE MIDDLE AGES SERBIAN RULERS FROM ZETA RULED OVER THIS TOWN, DEVELOPING IT TO ITS CLIMAX. BETWEEN THE BEGINNING OF THE 15TH CENTURY AND 1571 THE VENETIANS RULED IN THE TOWN ONLY TO BE TAKEN OVER BY THE DEFEATED TURKS WHO SETTLED HERE 400 ALGERIAN PIRATES. FOR TWO CENTURIES THESE PIRATES WERE SINKING SHIPS, PLUNDERING, KILLING AND TRADING PEOPLE. ...NOT FAR FROM ULCINJ THERE IS THE LARGEST BEACH ON THE YUGOSLAV COAST OF THE ADRIATIC, MADE UP OF MEDICINAL RADIOACTIVE SANDS.

OLD BAR. ON THE SPURS OF THE RUMIJA MOUNTAIN WE FIND THE RUINS OF THE MEDIEVAL STRONGHOLD WHICH HAD ITS HEYDAY IN THE DAYS OF THE NEMANJIĆ DYNASTY. IN THE 15TH CENTURY THE FORTIFICATION WAS CONQUERED BY VENETIANS, AND IN THE 16TH CENTURY INVADED AND TAKEN BY TURKS WHO HELD IT UNTIL 1878. ITS GHOSTLIKE RUINS LEAVE AN INDELIBLE IMPRESSION UPON THE VISITOR, ABOVE ALL AT DAYBREAK AND SUNSET.

ŠAVNIK. THE MOUNTAINOUS LANDSCAPES OF CRNA GORA (MONTENEGRO) SURPRISE US EVERY NOW AND THEN WITH UNEXPECTED VISTAS. ON ONE SIDE OF THE CANYON THERE ARE CLIFFS AND ROCKS AND ON THE OTHER A PLATEAU OF PASTURES.

THE CIJEVNA. ONE OF THE MOST BEAUTIFUL MONTENEGRIN RIVERS FLOWS QUIETLY IN ITS COURSE CUT INTO BARREN ROCKS. BUT WHEN SPRING RAINS COME THIS CAPRICIOUS RIVER RISES RAPIDLY, CARRYING IN ITS COURSE WHATEVER IT MEETS IN ITS WAY.

CRNO LAKE, THE MOST BEAUTIFUL OF THE SIXTEEN GLACIAL LAKES IN THE DURMITOR RANGE. THE LUSCIOUS CONIFER TREE FOREST
AND THE STEEP ROCKS ARE WONDERFULLY REFLECTED IN THESE TWO BLACK MOUNTAIN PEARLS.

ON THE LEFT: OSTROG MONASTERY. WITHDRAWING BEFORE TURKS, MITROPOLIS VASSILIUS BUILT AND FORTIFIED THIS MONASTERY IN THIS VERTICAL CLIFF, 900 METRES ABOVE SEA LEVEL, WHERE ALL TURKISH ATTEMPTS TO CONQUER IT REMAINED ONLY DISASTROUS FAILURES.

BRIDGE ON THE LEVER TARA: 366 METRES LONG, 150 METRES HIGH, THUS BEING ONE OF THE HIGHEST IN EUROPE. IT WAS BUILT BY ENGINEER LAZAR JAUKOVIĆ WHO ALSO DESTROYED IT ON INSTRUCTIONS OF THE SUPREME COMMAND OF THE PEOPLE'S LIBERATION ARMY. IN RETALIATION THE OCCUPYING FORCES ORDERED THE EXECUTION OF LAZAR JAUKOVIĆ ON THE BRIDGE. AFTER LIBERATION THE BRIDGE WAS RE-BUILT IN ITS ORIGINAL SHAPE.

VIEW OF THE ST. NIKOLA ISLET IN FRONT OF BUDVA AND PART OF THE TYPICAL MONTENEGRIN COAST WHICH — APART FROM SOME SETTLEMENTS — STEEPLY GOES DOWN TO THE SEA AND FORMING COUNTLESS BAYS WITH SAND AND GRAVEL BEACHES, AND WITH BARE AND VERTICAL CLIFFS ON HEAD-LANDS.

ANOTHER VIEW OF THE ROMANTIC CRNO LAKE, UNDER THE SNOW-CAPPED PEAKS OF DURMITOR.

KOTOR. VIEW OF THE RAMPARTS, 20 METRES HIGH, WHICH LEAD FROM THE FORTIFICATION OVERLOOKING THE SEA TO THE FORTRESS OF THE TOP OF THE MOUNTAIN UNDERNEATH THE STEEP LOVĆEN MOUNTAIN RANGE. AT THE FOOT OF THE MOUNTAIN WE FIND A TYPICAL MEDITERRANEAN SMALL TOWN WITH NUMEROUS SACRAL AND LAY BUILDINGS IN ROMANESQUE, GOTHIC, RENAISSANCE, AND BAROQUE STYLES.

CETINJE. WITHDRAWING BEFORE TURKS IN 1484 IVAN CRNOJEVIĆ BUILT A MONASTERY IN THIS MOUNTAIN VALLEY, AND A CASTLE IN ORLOV KRŠ. THE TURKS DESTROYED THE MONASTERY SEVERAL TIMES AND BURNT THE CASTLE DOWN THREE TIMES. BUT THEY WERE RE-BUILT AGAIN ONLY TO BECOME MORE RESOLUTE IN THEIR DEFENCE OF FREEDOM "UNTIL OUR OR TURKISH EXTIRPATION". THIS TOWN MUSEUM WAS THE CAPITAL OF MONTENEGRO FOR CENTURIES, THE SEAT OF ARCHBISHOPS, DUKES, AND KINGS.

VIRPAZAR ON THE COAST OF SKADAR LAKE WHICH WAS FORMED BY STEADY SUBSIDENCE OF GROUND. THE WATER FROM THE RIVERS FLOODED WHAT USED TO BE A FERTILE PLAIN AND MADE A VAST AREA ROUND THE LAKE UNFERTILE AND SWAMPY. THE ADRIATIC HIGHWAY AND RAILWAY LINE CROSS THE LAKE.

VIEW OF THE WESTERN PART OF SKADAR LAKE AND THE ROMANTIC ESTUARY OF THE CRNOJEVIĆA RIVER, SQUEEZED IN AND INTER-
SECTED BY GENTLE HILLS AT THE FOOT OF HUGE MOUNTAIN RANGES.

THE ORIENTAL BRIDGE ON THE CRNOJEVIĆA RIVER ADDS A SPECIAL CHARM TO THIS ROMANTIC VALLEY. ON THE ROCKY HILL ABOVE
THE VILLAGE OBOD IS SITUATED WHERE THE FIRST SLAV PRINTING PRESS WAS FOUNDED, ONLY 39 YEARS AFTER GUTENBERG'S INVENTION

VIEW OF ONE OF THE GULFS OF BOKA KOTORSKA, THE LARGEST AND MOST BEAUTIFUL MEDITERRANEAN FIORD. PIERRE LOTI WROTE ON BOKA KOTORSKA IN 1880: »SLOWLY I AM GETTING USED TO THIS HUGE MASS OF STONE WHICH RISES STRAIGHT TOWARDS THE SKIES, TO THE MAGNIFICENT BEAUTY OF THIS PART OF THE EARTH WHICH IS REMINISCENT OF THE HORRID REMAINS OF CHAOS".

THE CHAOTIC STONE SEA OF KOMOVO AND PROKLETIJE SHOULD SERVE AS FAREWELL FROM THE WILD, MAGNIFICENT, ROMANTIC AND HEROIC LANDSCAPES OF MONTENEGRO.

Man constantly returns to the sea coasts from which he once parted with so much difficulty. It is not only chance that almost all civilizations were born and died out on the coasts of the seas; neither was it chance that man stayed so long near the water, conveying himself from one coast to the other, constantly altering the coast-line of all seas and oceans, and creating unusual shapes, which could never have been formed by waves, rain, wind or volcanos. He built and moulded the face of the land. These local areas, distinctive with creations, man lined along all coasts, died on the coasts, and the work of his hand died with him. In such a way thousands of generations and civilizations were born and died on all coasts of the world.

And so started this, perhaps the richest, civilization, which germinated on the humus of the previous ones, on the east coast of the Mediterranean depression, which during the legendary Flood was filled with blue water, bluer than any other. This warm and irresistably tempting water became the cradle of enchanting childhood of this country's civilization. Standing at the edge of these mysterious and threatening waters, these frightened ancestors filled the dark depths with Gods and ghosts, phantoms and monsters, Poseidons and Leviathans, joy and suffering. And when habit drove away fear, they took a tree-trunk and set off across the rough and inhospitable surface, carrying with them some of the human knowledge and experience.

And so before five or six thousand years on the east coast of the Adriatic — that marvellous stretch of the vast Mediterranean lake, like a wedge penetrating from the south-east to the north-west into the heart of the European continent — on that incomparably indented lacy coast-line one can find many traces of the neolithic aboriginals.

Patterned and coloured ceramics, decorated with rich ornaments, are not only witness of the highly developed culture, but also of firm and durable connections with other old Mediterranean cultures. A design carved on a clay pot shows that a developed skill of sailing was known by these aboriginals of the Adriatic coast.

At the beginning of the second millennium A. D., Indo-European Illyrians came to this coast as carriers of the Bronze Age culture, and later of the Iron Age culture. Fortified settlements, situated on the hill-tops, surrounded with concentric walls, tools, weapons, jewellery and money, monumental stony sculptured figures, developed seamanship, live trading, building of towns and the beginnings of organized state communities, eloquently speak of the transition from prehistory to history.

And history during the coming two thousand years will record thousands of dramas, which constantly took place on the Adriatic waves. Ships after ships; those with boat-hooks and war-beaks, those with guns and machine-guns, those with sails and oars and those using steam or crude-oil, cursed galleys and still more cursed cruisers — ships on the water, and under the water, for two thousand years meant death and blood, and made the sea violent. Illyrians, Greeks and Romans, Goths, Avars and Slavs, Byzantines, Franks, Saracens, and Normans, Spaniards, Napolitans, and Venetians, Hungarians, Mongols and Turks, Italians, Austrians and French, crusaders and knightly orders, pirates, venturins and uskocs, dukes, kings, czars and popes, revolted slaves and sailors, tyrannized people and classes, christians and heathens, bogomils and moslems ... all killed and were killed on these playful blue waves which seem only created for careless tourists.

But all ships did not sail under the flag of death and loaded with gunpowder and killing steel. On the contrary, there were more of those with cargos of bread and salt, silk and spices, wood and marble. For two thousand years the Adriatic was a hugh trading road which stretched to all parts of the world in those days, and from all parts brought wealth, storing it on the coast in the form of most luxurious buildings which survived the centuries.

Despite of destroying wars, fires and epidemics, the persistent inhabitants of the Adriatic coast started anew from the ruins.

The life of this culture, from Illyrians and Greek colonists until to-day has carried on to this day.

In the 4th century Greeks founded many colonies (Issa, Pharos, Tragurion, Epition, Salona etc.) on the coast and on the Adriatic islands, and gave their settlements the characteristic form of antique urban life. The remains of monumental buildings, fortresses, temples, terracotta tanagra statuettes, a bronze head and a marble relief of »Kairos«, represents the beginning of the millennium old development of antique art on this Adriatic coast.

Wishing to dominate the whole Mediterranean the Romans started to invade Illyria during the Punic Wars, and finished during the rule of Augustus. In a few centuries they erected a great number of large and splendid towns, and in hundreds of sheltered bays and coves overgrown with fragrent Adriatic vegetation, they built many villas and summer residences. And these villas and residences of Roman veterans and idle patricians eloquently speak of the beauty and elevation of the coast.

In spite of all the merciless devastations and incendiarism during the great emigration of people, even from the whole Roman Empire, there is not such an area with so many monuments of imperial architecture: reliefs, sculptures, mozaics and ornamented sarcophagi, temples and temple ruins, theatres and other public buildings, the magnificent amphitheatre in Pula, and the still more magnificent Diocletian Palace in Split.

Victorious Christianity, from the beginning of the 4th to the end of the 6th century, established a great number of basilicas in all Roman towns and settlements — wonderful monuments of late-Antique architecture. Excavated foundations and many preserved details most convincingly speak of this period.

Justinian's raid on Italy (535—540) opened up a new period of late-Antique architecture on this coast. Euphrasius's Basilica in Poreč, one of the almost completely preserved monuments from that period in the world, is just one example.

At the beginning of the 7th century Slavs with their ally the Avars destroyed all that was possible to destroy. Only a few forgotten specimens and large buildings remained, which still to-day tell us about the rich life and the violent death of a great and valuable culture.

Avars withdrew, and the Slavs remained as masters of this coast, accepted Christianity and one part of a dying and changing culture. They started building their poor, but in the history of architecture unique buildings of so-called old-Croatian architecture. Nowhere in the world were so many monuments left from the pre-Romanesque period, as on this coast. Later the Romanesque style accentuated the development of architecture, and it has existed through all evolutional periods, early and late Gothic, Renaissance and Baroque, up until to-day in the steeples; the unique verticals of all coastal towns and villages.

A whole millennium passed by with the insecure rule of Slavic states, interventions and control of foreign powers (Spain, Venice, Hungary, Austria, Turkey etc.), piracy and rebellions, victories and defeats. From the 15th century until Napoleon the whole of the Adriatic coast was ruled by Venice; with the exception of part of the Croatian coast, the Republic of Dubrovnik and part of the Montenegrin coast. This narrow coastal strip, which was under the rule of Venice, and under the flag of independent Dubrovnik — and as such to a certain degree secure although lying along the threatening Turkish border — slowly but surely developed its culture with all its aspects: literature, theatrical art, architecture, painting and sculpture, handicraft, and from woodcarving and filigree work to tapestry and embroidery.

No, this is not a deserted or innocent coast, pure and untouched, nor is this sea only dreamy water under shimmering moonbeams. Here, for thousands of years lived man, suffered and slaved, fell and rose again. He built monuments for himself, and in memory of himself. A memory in stone, lamented by the cobalt sea — blue with a hint of red — violet iridescent water coloured by blood.

From the Renaissance town of Kopar to the high uncanny teeth of Turkish Stari Bar and Ulcinj, the base on Ali Hodža, — that mad Islamic pirate who fought against all Mediterranean ships including the Turkish — large and small towns lie one next to the other, of which every one has its thousands of years old history. And nowhere on this coast can be found 10 kilometres without a stony monument, dating from Antique up until to-day. Monuments, one next to the other, as if welded and grown together into one unique harmonious, carefully balanced urban whole. Dubrovnik is the best known and most wonderful example, an example without a flaw, to which can be added without shame — although much smaller — the stony pearl, Trogir. The Antique heart of Split and Pula, late-Antique Poreč, the Romanesque complex of Zadar, Rab and a whole row of towns large and small, flowery Gothic and Renaissance, equally harmoniously alive and intermixed in sacred and secular buildings, border the blue dress of the sea with a wonderful white lace.

The edge of this white lace is not even as on the Italian side, but is indented and patterned with thousands of wonderful features. Large and small bays, coves and fiords, cut in the rock, or settled on beaches of white pebbles and sand in the scented shadow of Mediterranean vegetation, which exhibits itself, from the sparse spiky grass and undergrowth to the thick forests of pine and jasmine.

This indented, lacy edge of the sea gives the Yugoslav coast an exceptional and unique world value. Although Yugoslavia has only a third of the Adriatic air-line, the actual amount of coastline in the country comes to four-fifths (78⁰/₀); in fact 6,116 kilometers of the whole Adriatic coast which has 7,867 kilometers. This coastal line is not only made up from bays, penetrating into the lime-stone mountains, which like a chain encloses the east side of the Adriatic, but also from 1,233 islands and islets scattered along the whole coast. In the beginning it was mentioned that veterans and idle Roman patricians built villas and summer resorts in many bays. These sober, rational, martial and so merciless people of Antique looked for small nooks of solitude and peace, enclosed bays, far away from the clash of swords and the noise of the Forum.

Engraved on a rock in the Živogoška Bay in the Makarska area, we can read the following inscription:

»Pressed by the edges of the bank's rugged rocks this stream of cold water runs away in torrents... one who lives in this country cannot find enough praise for its pleasant taste, and the occasional visitor for its richness. Hail Nymph, you who condescended to visit my land and so make famous this place: you with this beneficial spring glorified my estate, and I, Licinian, its owner, wish to praise you with this »poem«.

This extract from an epigram of a sober, rational man of Antique is an extract from the soul of people from all times. Everyone carries within himself an irresistible wish for appeasement in a secluded bay, near a cold spring, with the murmuring of the stream, the wind and the sea. However much one denies it, with laughter and bluffs, one's intimate self, and only self, remains always melancholy, tender and lonely. Man from the very beginning has been affected by romance; in Antique times, in Renaissance times, and in these modern times. And in these Adriatic bays — on the coast and on the islands — man has since time immemorial built lonely abodes to feel alone and free in solitude, to be face to face, whisper to whisper with nature and the sea.

Romans, and Slavic dukes and kings, barefoot friars and magnificently clad bishops, Renaissance gentlemen — home and foreign, Venetian governors and Austrian generals... all of them erected courts, castles, citadels and summer resorts, and they all stood on the edge of the sea listening to the murmur and crash of the waves and whistle of the wind, absorbing the silver beams of the moon they merged into the infinitely deep and clear Mediterranean star-lit sky. They all went sailing in boats and small ships, rocked by them, they idly chattered the days away, and when the sea was tranquil they watched the bottom, patterned with strange shapes, colours and life.

In spite of this uncertain time with the eternal fear of attack from pirates, Turks or Continental raiders, man never stopped going to the sea, where he fortified himself or retreated into natural shelters; in caves whose entrances were secured with an impenetrable wall. For instance, man from Rogoznica (Omiš) could have built on inaccessible mountain rocks, but he went down towards the sea and withdrew into the cave on the steep cliff near Rus-kamen... not only because of security.

The smell of iodine and salt, the everlasting murmuring of mysterious waters, which constantly attract one near them, caused many to run away from the rush and bustle of town life. For that reason monks built their monasteries outside the walls of the fortified towns, ecclesiastic and secular Medieval gentlemen withdrew into castles, and ordinary people retreated to the field cottages — which were not just for guarding the fields — and built houses in isolation, or here and there around the town, although inside the town walls there was always enough room for building.

And what does modern man do, who is not imperilled by the sudden attack of raiders? What does this proud master of the land, sea and air, do; this warrior who seriously is ready to actually conquer the solar system? This demigod cannot condescend to imitate his wild and immobile ancestors with their melancholy, romantic contacts with nature; to withdraw into an isolated house, to listen to the murmur of the sea and wind, to smell the iodine and salt, to watch the star-lit sky and with a spear to kill fish...

No! He doesn't withdraw into caves and castles, but in small week-end cottages and even smaller canvas tents, which he moves from place to place like a bee from flower to flower. This nomad of the automobile age never uses a spear to kill fish, but has an underwater gun. He doesn't sing sentimental songs, but turns on the transistor. He never goes on foot, neither on horse-back, nor does he travel in a romantic coach, but rushes along in trains, cars and metal birds, rushing in flocks... Where? — To the sea.

And what does he do at the sea? He bathes in the water and sunshine, eats fish and drinks wine, sits in a motor-boat and cuts across the open sea. He wanders around rocky islets and deserted islands, adjusts his under-water mask and for hours and hours enjoys watching the bottom of the sea, patterned with strange shapes, colours and life. He admires the cliffs, pounded by the waves, admires the temples, fortresses, palaces and towns, built over a period of thousands of years, and he attempts to capture their beauty through the cold and curious eye of his camera. He rests in the shadow of the rich Mediterranean vegetation, and looks for lonely coves where he can bathe as nature intended, giving himself up completely to the sun and the sea. And when night falls, dancing. After the dancing, that romantic walk by the sea, along the paths soft with millions of pine-needles. And the heart beats with ardent blood and the sun-burnt skin glows, while moonlight floods the vast expanse of water and animates the rocks. The cricket chirps, from the distant illuminated gardens of the summer resort the sound of gay music is heard which intermingles with the sound from the transistor, and with hundreds of sweet, whispered and insignificant words.

Isn't this just as romantic as the romance of our ancestors? No! — angrily answers the modern man — It's recreation! Apart from this »recreation«, which thirstily absorbs all that our romantic ancestors enjoyed, and all the countless beauties of the east Adriatic coast (from Plava laguna of Poreč, Limski kanal, Zavratnica, the wonderful Kornati group and scented Elafitski islands, to the unique Boka Kotorska, and the 12 kilometres long wide and sandy beach, from the bare stony bays to those covered with green vegetation, from a thousand pebbled to a thousand sandy beaches, from neolithic caves to confortable skyscraper hotels); apart from all these beauties, there is something else which irresistibly draws man: —

Sun and warmth.

The Adriatic is a huge storage unit for heat. The east coast absorbs sixteen times more heat energy than inland on the same line of latitude. Armed with milliards of stored kiloca-lories the Adriatic confidently waits for winter, when the border of snow is pushed high up above the coast. From Kopar to Ulcinj the January temperature is approximmately 4^0 to 9^0 centigrade, and in July is 22^0 to 27^0 centigrade. At the end of winter the temperature on the open sea in the north-west Adriatic is 7.5^0 centigrade, and in the south-east is 13.5^0 centigrade.

Infrequent rain or overcast skies, plenty of sunshine and warm southern winds in the central and south Adriatic, cause mild winters, and even some days convenient for bathing. And in the summer the »Maestral« (south-west wind) refreshes the whole coast every day.

The sea always remains the same; in summer when the whole coast is covered with a chain of unclothed and thirsty human ants, and in late autumn when the motorized nomads withdraw and only the irrecoverable romantics remain; when the sea uncovers more of itself. Great and splendid performances are shown to the lonely stroller. The air becomes heavy over the sea and full of the smell of dying leaves, and unfolding the warm and damp wings of the south wind, begins with 30 metres wide waves to slowly but surely pound the already cruelly beaten rocks. And a melancholy falls over all, sweet, quiet, sorrowful, chateaubriandlike; falls this melancholy merging into the white foam, like a rich ermine border of this blue watery gown.

And then the frozen blue sky opens, and snowy whiteness covers the ridge and slopes of the vast mountain range, and the sharp, dry bura-gale whistles, and man sits under a cliff, basking in the sunshine of this sheltered spot and watching the open sea, white, quite white from the short, high waves leaping up and crashing down again, like piles of splintered glass, or scattered pearls.

Then comes spring, early spring, almost in the middle of the continental winter, and all is white again, but no longer with the spray of water, but with thousands of blossoming crowns of the Mediterranean fruit trees. Deep blue sea, deep blue sky — separated by fluffy white life.

And once again it's summer, and the unromantic man of to--day, this master of land, sea and air, conqueror of outer space, rushes towards this lacy, unique Adriatic coast, from all parts of Europe — even from the other side of the Atlantic...

Romance? Oh no! — It's recreation!

Ivan Raos

IS IT FROZEN SNOW AFTER ICY RAIN, SPLINTERED GLASS, OR THE FOAMING FURY OF THE SEA? IT MAKES NO DIFFERENCE. MAN RELAXES
AND DREAMS HIS NEVER-ENDING DREAM OF BEAUTY.

THE EXTRAORDINARY INDENTEDNESS OF
THE EASTERN COAST OF THE ADRIATIC
IS SOMETIMES SMOTHERED BY THE
LUSCIOUS MEDITERRANEAN VEGETATION,
IMPREGNATED WITH FRESHNESS AND THE
INTOXICATING FRAGRANCE OF THE SOUTH.

IN THE SHIFTING ROCKY MOUNTAINS, IN THE TREMBLING TRANSPARENT WATER WITH ITS POLISHED PEBBLES, AND THE DIGNIFIED SERIOUSNESS OF THE BIRDS MAN COMES IN LIKE A DISCORD.

THE IDENTICAL CURIOSITY OF MAN AND THE SEA: TO REACH WHATEVER IS POSSIBLE AND SATISFY THEMSELVES, OR JUST LEAVE AN IMPRESSION.

ALL OF A SUDDEN A PLAYFUL CLOUD APPEARS, STEALS THE SUNLIGHT AND WITH ITS FLIRTATIOUS BEAUTY MOMENTARILY COVERS THE ROCKS AND THE SEA.

OH, THESE PRETENTIOUS CLOUDS: "WE CAN GO UP OR DOWN, BROADEN AND FLOAT. LOOK AT US! FROM HORIZON TO HORIZON, FROM THE SEA TO THE SKY!" AND THE SEA KEEPS QUIET BECAUSE IT KNOWS THAT THE PUFFED CLOUDS COME AND GO, WHILE ONLY SHE IS STEADFAST AND ETERNAL.

IT PLEASED THE WIND TO CHANGE THE COLOUR OF THE BLUE SEA INTO SILVER.

IN THE WAR BETWEEN THE STONE AND THE SEA THERE IS AN OCCASIONAL TRUCE, PERHAPS ONLY TO GIVE THE ROCK A CHANCE TO LOOK INTO THE MIRROR BELOW TO UNDERSTAND THAT ANOTHER BATTLE HAS BEEN LOST.

BETWEEN THE MOLTEN SILVER AND THE GREY LINE OF THE HORIZON THE DARK OUTLINES OF THE GREEN BRIONI ISLANDS,

IN GENTLE WHIRLS THE WATER CIRCLES ROUND SMALL REEFS, BUT ONCE IT GETS FURIOUS IT WILL EASILY SPLASH OVER THESE
HUGE ROCKS

ON THE DEAD STONES OF KORNATI MAN PLANTED LIFE AND — SURPRISINGLY — THESE STONES KEPT IT ALIVE.

GIGANTIC SHELLS OR CLAMS? OR PERHAPS MYSTERIOUS FLYING SAUCERS SECRETLY SAILING OVER THE   HUSHED SEA?

THE SLENDER HEADLANDS OF KORČULA — WHICH BECAUSE OF ITS DENSE AND IMPASSABLE FORESTS WAS CALLED "CRNA" (BLACK) EVEN BY GREEKS AND ROMANS — AS ALWAYS LEISURELY AND PEACEFULLY DREAMING — IMPASSIVE EVEN WHEN THE UNREASONABLE SEA BECOMES THREATENING AND STORMY.

THE VERTICALLY STEEPING ROCKS DO NOT STOP JUST BELOW THE SURFACE BUT PIERCE THE DEEP BLUE SEA FOR TENS OF METRES.

BETWEEN THE ROCKY MASSES OF MOSOR AND DINARA THE CETINA HAS CUT A DEEP CANYON AND TAKING WITH IT THE PATIENTLY GROUND SAND INTO THE SEA, FROM WHICH SHALLOWS AND SAND-BANKS ARE FORMED.

THE BARREN, CRUEL AND INACCESSIBLE BIOKOVO FROM THIS DISTANCE, WITH ITS SOFT BACKGROUND OF THE SEA AND COVERED BY
A LAYER OF FLUFFY CLOUDS, SEEMS TO BECOME SOFTER AND TAMER.

A FINE MIST HAS FALLEN OVER RIJEKA AND THIS LARGE HARBOUR AND SHIP-BUILDING TOWN IS TRANSFORMED INTO A DELICATE AQUARELLE.

THE CLOUDS FORMED A REFLECTOR, AND THE DARK OUTLINES OF THE MONTENEGRIN LITTORAL HAVE ACQUIRED A NEW DIMENSION IN HALF-SHADOW.

THERE IS NO END OF THE PLAY BETWEEN THE LIGHT GREY STONES OF KORNATI AND THE CLEAR, TRANSPARENT, BLUE WATER.

MAN DECLARED WAR AGAINST THE ROCKS AND MEDITERRANEAN UNDERGROWTH; VINEYARDS FULL OF GRAPE CLUSTERS AND OLIVE GROVES KEEP AWAY THE BARRENNESS.

THE HEAVY, DAMP, MONOTONOUS SOUTHERN WIND ALWAYS FILLS US WITH A SWEET MELANCHOLY AND GLOOMY THOUGHTS OF TRANSITORINESS.

NO, THIS IS NOT A CANYON OF A KARST RIVER, BUT THE APPROXIMATELY FOUR KILOMETRE LONG MASLENIČKO ŽDRILO LINKING THE VELEBIT CHANNEL WITH THE NOVIGRAD SEA. WHAT A CONTRAST AND HARMONY BETWEEN THE MEEK WATER AND THE THREAT-ENING BARRENNESS OF THE VELEBIT CLIFFS.

AND SO ALONG THE WHOLE EASTERN COAST OF THE ADRIATIC INETERCHANGE VERTICAL CLIFFS EXPOSED TO THE DIRECT POUNDING
OF THE SEA AND SHARP ROCKS....

THE IDENTICAL CURIOSITY OF MAN AND THE SEA: TO REACH WHATEVER IS POSSIBLE AND SATISFY THEMSELVES, OR JUST LEAVE AN IMPRESSION.

ALL OF A SUDDEN A PLAYFUL CLOUD APPEARS, STEALS THE SUNLIGHT AND WITH ITS FLIRTATIOUS BEAUTY MOMENTARILY COVERS THE ROCKS AND THE SEA.

.... WITH SWEET CLOSED-IN PEBBLED AND SANDY BEACHES, BARE STONES WITH SMALL GROVES AND RICH MEDITERRANEAN VEGE-
TATION, BUT THE SEA REMAINS PERMANENTLY THE SAME: DEEP BLUE AND MYSTERIOUS.

WITHOUT A LEAF, WITHOUT A FLOWER, WITHOUT A BLADE OF GRASS, AND WITHOUT ANY SIGN OF LIFE ....LIKE A DISTANT SILENT PLANET.

IS THIS PURELY ACCIDENTAL OR IS IT AN UNAVOIDABLE CONDITION OF THE SEA THAT EVEN SHIPS MUST HAVE THE SKELETON OF A FISH?

ISLANDS AND MOUNTAINS EMERGED THE DEPTHS OF THE SEA. WATER WASHES AND EATS THEM AWAY UNTIL THEY ARE AGAIN COVERED. AND THEN AGAIN FROM THE DEPTHS OF THE WATER .... AND SO IN A CIRCLE, SEA AND ROCKS, UNTIL ONE OR THE OTHER CEASES. →

Today we know that man lived in Yugoslavia some fifty thousand years ago, that he warmed himself with fire, that he hunted animals and carved them with his stone knives. Remains of the dilluvial man of the Neanderthal type were found in the Hušnjak cave near Krapina in Hrvatsko Zagorje by Prof. Kramberger-Gorjanić. This forerunner of the present man was called »homo Krapiniensis«. After that followed darkness... several tens of thousands years of darkness. And yet in all these centuries and thousands of years man found warmth near his small fires, he loved and hated, he was raising new generations and was dying, he was killing and was being killed, he sang new songs, coined new words, new weapons and tools, he started cultivating his land, taming animals, building his small huts and whole civilisations... Slowly but persistantly man was striding forward to become the species that would grow so powerful and large that it would eventually populate all parts of the world, all known, and unknown continents and regions.

For many thousands of years man fought his way with a stone knife and an ax — they can be found all over Yugoslavia — until he found the fabulous metal called copper which enabled man to turn the wheel of history more rapidly.

The neolithic civilisation was thriving in Yugoslavia in its Mediterranean and continental versions. Numerous weapons, tools, and copper ornaments, as well as remains of foundries, and a great number of accessories made of ceramics, are sufficient evidence of the fact that the people of what is today Yugoslavia were not isolated even several thousand years ago, but that they carried on trade with a number of countries at the Aegeian and Ionian seas, Egypt, Syria, etc. The neolithic tribes in the interior were in touch with all countries in the Danube area, and the famous amber way crossed Yugoslavia.

After the Illyrians, the main representatives of the copper and early iron civilisations, were subjugated, their civilisation disappeared together with their tombs and buildings in the interior of the country. The well-organised, statesmanlike and rational Romans spread the splendour of their insurpassable civilisation all over Yugoslavia. Neolithic caves, log--houses, primitive stone houses, even fortifications, were replaced by the wonderful Roman buildings — perfect in shape and functional design — in all major well-organised towns (Pola, Jadera, Scadrona, Salonae, Narona, Siscia, Mursa, Singidunum, Vininatium, Vanona, Naissus, Scupi, Stobi, and tens of others). To a twentieth century man it seems that Romans were able to build magnificent buildings without any tools — buildings that have survived thousands of years.

But Rome was in its decline and the primitive man was violating the *limes* of the Empire in hordes, precipitating the disintegration of the highly developed civilisation in Roman towns. Various invaders attacked the Empire, destroying whatever came in their way. The last to come were the Slavs with their masters the Avars who were destroying whatever was still to be found in this part of the country. Later, when the Avars withdrew, the Slavs started re-building and restoring the country — slowly, painfully, and patiently. Instead of the amphitheatres, temples, palaces, and villas, the Slav conquerors were erecting tiny old Croatian chapels of raw, almost unhewn stone, one-room huts built of stone and timber, and they fortified their settlements with roughly built walls and wooden pillars — in general one can say that five centuries after the destruction of the Roman civilisation they were at the Illyrian stage of development.

Just when they were consolidating, when they were developing their civilisation in their own states which became very powerful, the Turks invaded the country of the Southern Slavs to remain there for several centuries.

Since then the country had pursued the pattern of different cultures. The towns and other settlements in the eastern part were developing under the strong influence of Islamic culture, while the Slavs in the western regions and in the coastal belt were under considerable influence of West European and Mediterranean cultures. Most Southern Slavs became feudal slaves of the Mohammedan, and the smaller part of the Austrian and Venetian masters.

And what could slaves create? Without freedom, without any power, without financial means, naked and bare-foot, hungry and ill, stretched between the stake and ax, the rack and gallows. What can a naked man create — who is persecuted like a wild animal and who concentrates all his strength, talent and instincts on efforts to preserve his poor life? Nothing.

And yet he was creating. And this is his magic power. He had no money to build an Acropolis or Colosseum, Cheops' pyramids, Salamon's temple, or Semiramis' hanging gardens — and still he built both an Acropolis and a Colosseum: for five centuries he was stringing one verse after another, one song after another, blending sorrow with expectations, memories of old glory with hopes in resurrection and regained freedom. This enslaved and outlawed man composed thousands of songs and millions of verses, incomparably more beautiful and more numerous than any other people in the world. Illiterate, he preserved his poetic word, carrying it on from one generation to another, from one memory to another... for five hundred years. Blind fiddlers were walking from one village to another, from one church feast to another, singing their songs accompanied by the sounds of strings. These songs fascinated a great number of people at the beginning of Romanticism, including Goethe, who translated one of the most beautiful folk ballads, the »Hasanaginica«.

In addition to this invaluable treasury of lyric and epic poetry, in addition to hundreds of tales, jokes, riddles and anecdotes, this enslaved Slav people was singing its songs and dancing its magic lyrical and heroic dances for centuries. How many nuances can be found in the large spectrum, ranging from the lively Slovene songs to the deep sadness of Macedonian compositions, from the gay rhythm of Međimurje on a canvas of light nostalgia, to the painful melancholy of the Orient in the Bosnian »sevdalinka« songs: Croatian, Serbian, and Macedonian ensembles of folk songs and dances, with their wealth of rhythm, movement and costume, as well as their subdued sorrow, still fascinate spectators from all continents. These dances were not only expressing joy, entertainment, and occasional festive moods, but they were also the expression of deep sorrow and pain, the expression of defiance and threat.

This enslaved man had very limited materials for the expression of his visual inclinations: wool and flax, wood and clay, iron and copper. He created his costumes from wool and flax, and they were so vivid and original that practically in each village they were a new version. Well-balanced in cut and colours, checkered by a variety of ornaments, frequetly enriched by wonderful lacework, they were telling evidence on the visual taste of this primitive and illiterate man. From wood, stone, and clay he made houses and furniture, tools and dishes, as well as musical instruments, ornamenting them with a variety of patterns, reliefs, heads of animals and men, and other figures. He wrought iron weapons and tools, made pots and ornaments of copper, and embellished his rifles with rich graphic ornaments.

Thus man created his own great works of culture, creating even when his shirt and his last piece of bread were taken away — but his creative spirit was never destroyed.

In addition to nameless folk artists in villages, a great number of important artists and scholars were active in towns, expanding the horizons of national and European culture. Since Humanism and the Renaissance the peoples of Yugoslavia have given Europe and the world a considerable number of personalities who have added many a bit to the mosaic of European art and scientific thought. It will do to mention Marulić, Flacius, Križanić, Juraj Dalmatinac, the optician Gethaldus, the atomist Ruđer Bošković, the physicist Tesla, the linguist Karadžić, the poets Njegoš and Mažuranić in the past centuries, and the contemporary sculptor Meštrović and the Nobel-prize winners Ružička and Andrić, to realise the share of the peoples of Yugoslavia in the structure of world culture.

The liberation from the Turkish rule and feudalism did not improve the plight of the people who vere given some kind of spurious freedom. The country was devastated, the industry just in the throes of birth — and mostly owned by foreigners — the population rising steadily ... which meant the beginning of migration to the more developed countries of Europe and America. Those who were not able or did not want to look for bread abroad built houses, bred cattle, cultivated land exactly in the same way as their fathers and grandfathers were doing: petrified in the flow of time. Civilisation touched only the towns which developed in one way or another. And it was these towns that gave the impulse

to the general economic development: they were erecting new industries, exploiting natural resources, organising the building of roads and railway lines which in their turn contributed to the expansion and modernisation of agriculture and forestry, thus slowly reducing the percentage of wilderness and spreading civilisation, the civilisation of the machine. It took man thousands of years to make the first fire, tens of thousands of years to make the first nedle and another tens of thousands to thread the needle through its eye. How many thousands of generations from one small discovery to another! And then, as if by some wonder, within a century and a half — between the first groaning locomotive and today — man covered the whole globe with railway lines, filled the roads with motor cars, crowded the air with airplanes and space-ships, and superseded the hard and slow manual work by rapid stream-lined machines which are turning into a serious threat, to conquer eventually their creator — man himself.

If we take into account that the Southern Slavs wasted their forces for five centuries to free themselves from foreign domination (Turkish, Austria, Venetian, etc.), then we shall understand the reason of their technical and economic backwardness before the collapse of the Austro-Hungarian Empire in 1918. United after that collapse in their young state, they unfortunately wasted most of their energy in internal struggles and national frictions. The little that was erected in those years was again destroyed in the Second World War. Taking advantage of the most extreme representatives of national intolerance, the conquerors succeeded in turning the country into a scene of murder and robbery. The results were horrid: almost half of the villages and towns were destroyed and burnt down, while the casualties amounted to over 1.5 million killed, out of a population of 16 million! The peoples who attained national freedom after so many centuries of slavery did not want any new foreign masters. Gathered round Marshal Tito and Communistic Party they started the unequal fight against the occupying power, persisting heroically until the liberation of their country and the establishment of socialism.

After liberation the socialist citizens of Yugoslavia rolled up their sleeves and started building their desolate country, opening the door wide open to industrialisation and mechanisation. At first they started taming rapid mountain streams, abundant in this country, and turning their futile and frequently destructive power into a beneficial force. They erected large water power stations (Jablanica, Mavrovo, Split, Dubrovnik, and many others, including the latest super giant at the Danube in the Đerdap gorge — just under construction), they checkered the country with pylons, bringing electric light to the remotest and most backward parts of the country ...... Megawatts were rising steadily, they were doubled and in places reached three times as much electric power as in previous years, thus giving a powerful push forward to the development of light and heavy industry.

Derricks were rising in new oil-fields, compresors were drilling holes into the earth in search of coal, iron, copper, and silver, cone-like furnaces were rising, halls of ironworks, machine manufacturers, steam engine, locomotive and motor--car factories were being expanded. Looms were multiplying, rivers of dyestuff were flowing and thousands of tons of plastics were bending. Shipyards were erected which have been constructing all kinds of coastal and ocean-going vessels. The network of railway lines and asphalt roads has been steadily increasing. The number of sports and recreation grounds is increasing and so is the number of hotels and motels on the coast of the Adriatic.

Round the old town cores man has been hurriedly erecting new housing estates and in many cases whole new towns. 30 per cent of our peasant population has been absorbed by towns and industry in the last twenty years. The backward people are thirsty for knowledge and culture; the number of illiterates is shrinking, while the percentage of those with high qualifications and university degrees is steadily rising — Yugoslavia takes the third place in the world in the number of students. Yugoslav arts and literature are penetrating various parts of the world and science is rising on its feet; the great number of institutes, ranging from humanistic to technical and atomic establishments, have been producing ever more noteworthy results.

This man, this active and dynamic man is viewing himself and his great work, achieved within such a short time, with justified pride.

But there is another man who has remained faithful to nature, to the soil, to the forest and the barren stone, the man who takes his cattle across the river on a raft, who transports wood from the mountains to warm himself by his primitive hearth in a one-room hut, the man who lives exactly as people did live for centuries, and following their instincts in all details. He still lives in shabby stone and wooden houses covered by slabs, straw and shingles, he still cooks on a hearth over which hang copper pots, and he still uses the tools used by his greatparents. He still weaves his rich costumes, still dances his rings, he sings his joyful and sentimental songs and recites from memory heroic verses of the past.

As if defying civilisation.

But this defiance is useless. Civilisation makes irresistible progress. Machines have conquered all ploughfields in plains. Tractors and combines have superseded plouhmen and their faithful assistants: horses and oxen, while the radio and television sets have replaced fiddles and folk flutes, modern dances have brought the traditional rings to an end, and pop tunes have succeeded old sevdalinka songs. Rapid and inexpensive traffic communications are linking the villages with towns, and the villages are assuming the appearance of towns. The new townlike appearance is not manifested only in the erection of up-to-date houses and blocks of flats, but also in furniture, household goods and gadgets, in the health service, cultural and communal facilities, and also in the variety of economic activities. Agriculture is not any more the only activity of the people in farming regions. In some parts of the country, above all in Slovenia, there is practically in every village a small industrial plant, a workshop, a repair shop, and tourist facilities.

Only very high up, on inaccessible and frequently impassable mountain peaks, in mountains where there are no roads, civilisation has not succeeded in leaving its roots. But even here its feelers are present. A new school has been erected, a new doctor has arrived, and together with them newspapers, radio and television .... merchants are expanding the number of their branch offices and the range of commodities, local authorities are doing their best to take full advantage of the raw materials that can be found in their territory and to employ all possible manpower. Our time is the age of speed, the age of rapid exchange of material and spiritual goods. In the history and pre-history of mankind several civilisations lived simultaneously whtiout any interference, sometimes even one not knowing about the other. Today one new discovery spreads all over the world within a few years. Today the whole of mankind builds one united civilisation, at least in its material aspect. It will be perhaps only the spirit of some peoples that will shape the common achievements of our material culture, of our atomic civilisation, in their own individual way.

Ivan Raos

A FEW KNOTTY POSTS, SEVERAL UNHEWN LATHS JOINED WITH STRIPS OF WOOD, AND MAN CAN TAKE HIS FLOCK OF SHEEP ACROSS THE WATER. FOR CENTURIES THIS WAS THE WAY HOW IT WAS DONE, AND SO IT WOULD HAVE REMAINED IF THE NEW TORRENTS OF CIVILISATION DID NOT TAKE MAN TO NEW AND BRIGHTER SHORES.

CRAMPED UP FOR ROOM IN THE SQUEEZED MEDITERRANEAN SETTLEMENTS, MAN — WITH LITTLE MONEY AND PRIMITIVE EQUIPMENT — MANAGED TO ORGANISE HIS BASIC FACILITIES. THE TINY TERRACE IS USED FOR LAUNDERING AND DRYING CLOTHES, FOR AIRING BED-CLOTHES, FOR SUNNING AND A PEACEFUL SIESTA AFTER LUNCH, FOR FRYING FISH AND EVEN FOR SLEEP IN HOT SUMMER NIGHTS.

FROM MATERIALS THEY THEMSELVES HAVE WOVEN, THE WOMEN FROM THE ENVIRONS OF DUBROVNIK HAVE CREATED THIS WELL-BALANCED, SIMPLE AND DISTINGUISHED COSTUME WHICH, AS IT SEEMS, REQUIRES SUCH A DIGNIFIED GAIT.

THE »TRUPICA« — A PRIMITIVE ONE-OAR BOAT — SERVES TO DESCENDANTS OF THE ONCE NOTORIUS PIRATES FROM THE NERETVA AS A MEANS OF TRANSPORT FOR PEOPLE AND MATERIAL, FOR AGRICULTURAL PRODUCE, INDUSTRIAL AND MARSH PLANTS. SKILFUL OARSMEN, THE NERETLJANI MOVE ON THE LARGE LAKES WITH EASE — LAKES ABOUNDING IN EEL, WILD DUCK AND OTHER ANIMALS.

LEFT TO HIMSELF AND THE WILDERNESS OF THE MOUNTAIN, MAN IS HELPING HIMSELF AS BEST HE CAN, PATIENTLY SUFFERING HARD-
SHIPS AS INEVITABLE PARTS OF LIFE, AS AN ANTITHESIS TO THE JOYS OF LIFE. VERY EARLY CHILDREN ARE TAUGHT TO TAKE
PART IN HARD WORK AND THIS MAKES THEM REALISE THAT THERE CAN BE NO FIRE WITHOUT FIREWOOD AND NO MILK WITHOUT
BREEDING COWS AND SHEEP.

ON THE LEFT: FOR CENTURIES MAN LIVED LIKE THIS, FOLLOWING THE INSTINCT OF HIS ANCESTORS WHICH HE NEVER INTENDED TO EXPAND. WITH TOOLS INHERITED FROM HIS PREDECESSORS HE WOULD BUILD HIS HOME, A FENCE ROUND HIS HOUSE, HE WOULD HANG A CAULDRON OVER HIS HEARTH TO PREPARE THE SAME FOOD IN THE SAME WAY AS HIS GREATFATHERS HAD DONE.

WOODEN TROUGHS BY THE BROOK, WOODEN UTENSILS, COPPER POTS AND HANDS CHAPPED FROM WASHING CLOTHES — THE SAME HANDS THAT HAD WOVEN THE CLOTH THEY ARE NOW WASHING.

VERY EARLY MAN LEARNT MOST OF THE RESOURCES THAT HELP HIM TO SURVIVE. MUCH BEFORE HE STARTED CULTIVATING LAND MAN KNEW HOW TO CATCH DEER AND BIRDS, OR FISH IN STREAMS AND ON FORDS .... AND THEN, AFTER LONG CENTURIES HE INVENTED THE NET.

ON THE RIGHT: A LONG TIME AGO, PROBABLY IN PRE-HISTORIC TIMES, THE CITIZENS OF OHRID CAUGHT FISH IN THE SAME WAY AND IN A BOAT THAT IS VERY MUCH LIKE THE ONE IN THE PICTURE. THE TECHNIQUE SERVED ITS PURPOSE PERFECTLY SO THE FISHERMEN DID NOT FIND IT NECESSARY TO IMPROVE IT. BUT THEY LEARNT ONE THING: THE CATCH WAS LARGER IN BIGGER NETS AND THEY STARTED ASSOCIATING THEMSELVES INTO LARGER GROUPS.

ON THE RIGHT: HERE, TOO, TIME MUST HAVE A STOP. THE BEASTS OF DRAUGHT HAVE BEEN DRIVEN UNDER THE THREATENING BAT-
TLEMENTS OF THE MEDIEVAL FORTRESS WHICH THEY MUST NOT ENTER. IS NOT THIS LIKE A SCENE FROM A HISTORICAL FILM IN
WHICH NOTHING REMINDS US OF OUR TIMES?

VERY EARLY MAN LEARNT THAT LIVE ANIMALS ARE MORE USEFUL THAN DEAD ONES AND HE STARTED TAMING THEM. EVEN TODAY
MAN KEEPS TAMED ANIMALS, HE USES THEIR WARMTH AND HE FEEDS ON THEIR MILK AND DRESSES IN THEIR FLEECE. HE ALSO
TRADES WITH THEIR PRODUCTS, THUS GETTING ACQUAINTED WITH PEOPLE FROM OTHER PARTS OF THE WORLD AND WITH DIFFERENT
CUSTOMS.

THE SKILFUL HANDS OF DALMATIAN FISHERMEN SWIFTLY HANDLE THIS NET DISCOVERING THE DAMAGE WHICH MUST BE MENDED BEFORE THEY GO FISHING AGAIN. THEIR GRAND AND GREATFATHERS DID THE SAME .... ONLY WITHOUT GLASSES.

EVEN A THOUSAND YEARS AGO NETS — ACTUALLY BASKETS CALLED »VRŠE« — WERE MADE IN THE SAME WAY FROM WILLOW TWIGS,
ADEQUATE FOR A MODEST CATCH, FOR LUNCH OR SUPPER, FOR THE MEALS OF ONE DAY.

THE INTOXICATING SOUTHERN SUN AND THE SEVERE GALES FORCED THE CITIZENS OF DALMATIA TO BUILD HOUSES WITH THICK WALLS, AND TO BUILD LONG STONE BENCHES IN PLACES THAT ARE PROTECTED FROM THE WIND; HERE PEOPLE SPEND MOST OF THEIR HOURS OF RELAXATION, SOMETIMES IN NOISY AND SOMETIMES IN COSY CONVERSATION.

KUMROVEC, MARSHAL TITO'S BIRTH-PLACE IN HRVATSKO ZAGORJE. PICTURESQUE WHITE HOUSES WITH DARK ROOFS OF STRAW, SHIN-
GLES OR TILES, WITH GABLES OF DARK WOOD JEALOUSLY WATCHING OVER THE INTIMATE HUMAN WARMTH OF PAST CENTURIES.

THE WHEEL, THE PRE-HISTORIC MOVER OF OUR CIVILISATION, FIRST TURNED BY BEASTS OF DRAUGHT, IS STILL TURNING ROUND IN ITS HISTORIC ORIGINAL FORM IN PICTURESQUE ŠUMADIJA.

SICKLES, AS OLD AS OUR CIVILISATION OF BREAD, ARE STILL REAPING, AND THE STACKS SHOW THAT THE HOOVES OF HORSES BEAT
OUT THE GRAINS OUT OF HUSKS.

THE RICH COSTUMES FROM DALMATINSKA ZAGORA, WOVEN, CUT, AND SOWN AT HOME, TESTIFY TO THE FACT THAT THIS WORLD HAS SUCCEEDED IN PRESERVING THE TRADITION OF FOLK ART AND MAINTAINED IT THROUGH CENTURIES.

THE ROMAN PILLAR IN ZADAR WATCHES IMPASSIVLEY THE BUSTLE OF THE MARKET WHICH HAS PRESERVED ALL THE CHARM OF THE PAST: OFFERING GOODS, HAGGLING, AND CHATTING.... HOW MUCH NEARER THIS IS TO MAN FROM SELF-SERVICE SHOPS WHICH HAVE, HOWEVER, IMPOSED THEMSELVES IN ALL LARGER TOWNS AS THE FASTER AND MORE MODERN WAY OF SUPPLYING CUSTOMERS

ON THE LEFT: THE ŽIČA MONASTERY. IN HIS ATTEMPT TO FIND A HIGHER MEANING TO LIFE MAN HAS TRIED TO DISSOCIATE HIMSELF FROM THE EARTH AND MATERIALISE HIS ENDEAVOURS AND DREAMS OF THE ELEVATED AND THE BEAUTIFUL. MEDIEVAL MAN TRIED TO PRESERVE HIS EXPERIENCE OF BEAUTY IN MONUMENTAL SACRAL BUILDINGS.

BREAD IS SO PRECIOUS THAT IN MANY PARTS THE CUSTOM HAS BEEN KEPT ALIVE TO LIFT THE PIECE OF BREAD THAT WOULD DROP TO THE GROUND, TO CLEAN IT, KISS IT, AND THEN EAT IT. THIS MEANS HOMAGE TO HARD HUMAN WORK, TO SOWING, HARVESTING, AND THRESHING FOLLOWED BY PATIENT DRYING OF WHEAT GRAINS.

ON THE LEFT: MAN CAN GET EVEN THROUGH IMPASSABLE STONE GORGES — MAN AND HIS DEVOTED FRIEND, LOADED WITH FIREWOOD.

HOW MUCH HUMAN AND ANIMAL ENERGY IS REQUIRED BY THESE DEAD MONTENEGRIN STONES AND WITH WHAT PALTRY RESULTS.

FOUR NAKED WALLS, A THATCH ROOF, METAL AND WOODEN BOWLS, IN THE HOUSE PERHAPS A TRAY AND TWO POTS.... AND YET, WHO CAN CLAIM THAT HE IS QUIETER THAN THIS WOMAN ON THE STONY ISTRIAN PLATEAU?

THE SLANTING ROOF REACHING THE GROUND ON THE SIDES, AND THE FRONT DOOR IN FRONT — A TYPICAL MONTENEGRIN HOUSE
EXPOSED TO THE WIND AND HEAPS OF SNOW. BACKWARDNESS? DEFYING THE FLOW OF TIME? OR PERHAPS LOVE FOR THE PAST?

ON THE LEFT: MARKET IN DUBROVNIK. IN THIS STONE PEARL OF THE MEDITERRANEAN, IN SPITE OF THE HUGE PRESSURE OF TOURISTS FROM ALL PARTS OF THE WORLD, THE LIFE OF THE LOCAL POPULATION HAS REMAINED MORE OR LESS UNCHANGED. BUT IS NOT THERE SOMETHING VALUABLE IN THIS SLOW FLOW OF TIME?

HOMO LUDENS. MAN'S NEED OF GAMES AND TESTING HIS STRENGTH IS AS OLD AS HUMANITY. EACH YEAR — COMMEMORATING THE VICTORY OVER THE TURKS IN 1715 — THE FAMOUS »SINJSKA ALKA« TAKES PLACE AT SINJ. THE WINNER IS THE HORSEMAN WHO HAS THE GREATEST NUMBER OF HITS IN THE CENTRE OF THE RING »ALKA«, WHILE GALLOPING PAST THE TARGET.

THE PAST BELONGS TO THE PAST. THE PEOPLE OF YUGOSLAVIA ARE ADAPTING THEMSELVES TO NEW WAYS OF LIVING AND EARN-ING MONEY. THESE GIRLS ARE NOT PICKING PEACHES IN A SMALL ORCHARD, BUT ON A HUGE PLANTATION.

MAN HAS INVENTED THE MACHINE THAT IS MUCH STRONGER THAN HE AND HIS BEASTS OF DRAUGHT. ANOTHER MAN REALISED VERY SOON THAT THE TRACTOR IS FASTER THAN ANIMALS, THAT A COMBINE REAPS FASTER THAN THE SICKLE AND THRESHES MORE EFFICIENTLY THAN HORSES' HOOVES. WITHOUT SENTIMENT HE TOOK PART WITH THE OLD PLOUGH, SCYTHE AND THE HORSE. 15,000 TRACTORS ARE MANUFACTURED IN YUGOSLAVIA ANNUALLY.

TOBACCO FIELD OF THE TOBACCO INSTITUTE AT PRILEP. MAN IS MAKING AN EVER RISING USE OF SCIENCE SO AS TO GET MORE OUT OF HIS SOIL. THANKS TO THESE TRENDS THE CROPS AND THE QUALITY OF MACEDONIAN TOBACCO HAVE CONSIDERABLY IMPROVED, AND IT IS IN GREAT DEMAND ON WORLD MARKETS.

HUGE METAL AND CONCRETE SILOS HAVE REPLACED THOUSANDS OF PEASANT BARNS.... THE MAN ON THE TOP OF THE SILO IS NOT AFRAID OF THESE ROLLERS BECAUSE HE FEELS HE IS THEIR MASTER.

ON THE LEFT: FOR TWO THOUSAND YEARS HUGE WHITE STONE BLOCKS HAVE BEEN EXPORTED TO MANY COUNTRIES AND TOWNS FROM THE QUARRIES IN THE ISLAND OF BRAČ. STONE IS NOT ANY MORE SHAPED BY MEANS OF WEDGES — HERE, TOO, MODERN TECHNICAL DEVELOPMENT HAS HAD ITS SAY.

SHIPYARD IN PULA. THE CROATS HAVE BEEN EXCELLENT SHIPBUILDERS SINCE ANCIENT TIMES. KING TOMISLAV (10TH CENTURY) HAD ONE OF THE LARGEST FLEETS OF HIS TIME: THE PIRATES FROM THE NERETVA AND OMIŠ, THE »USKOCI« FROM SENJ, THE SAILORS FROM HVAR, BUT ABOVE ALL CITIZENS OF DUBROVNIK BUILT SAILING BOATS WHICH IN THEIRS STURDINESS, EQUIPMENT AND SPEED WERE COMPETING WITH THE BEST SHIPS OF THEIR TIME. THIS OLD TRADITION HAS ACQUIRED GIGANTIC DIMENSIONS LATELY. YUGOSLAV SHIPYARDS ARE AMONG THE FIRST IN THE WORLD BY THE TONNAGE OF THEIR PRODUCTION (OVER 300,000 BRT).

THE HEAVY HAMMERS OF THE SMITHS IN THE PAST HAVE BEEN REPLACED BY THE SLIM ELECTRODE FOR WHICH NO FIRM MUSCLES ARE NEEDED, BUT ONLY DARK GLASSES FOR PROTECTION AGAINST THE INTENSE LIGHT.

THE MUSCLES OF THE MODERN MAN ARE FAR STRONGER THAN THOSE OF HERCULES — WITH EASE THEY CAN LIFT WHOLE PARTS
OF SHIPS WHICH ARE OFTEN HEAVIER THAN WHOLE SHIPS OF THE PAST; ONE MODERN SHIP COULD CARRY THE WHOLE FLEET OF
THEMISTOCLES.

ABOVE AND ON THE RIGHT: THE »3 MAJ« SHIPYARD IN RIJEKA. HERE YUGOSLAV SHIPBUILDERS BUILD ALL KINDS OF VESSELS: PAS-
SENGER AND CARGO SHIPS, TRAWLERS, YACHTS, FLOATING DOCKS AND CRANES, TUGS, DREDGES, DIPPERS, TANKERS, AND BULK CARRIERS,
BETWEEN 7,000 AND 50,000 TONS.

DETAILS FROM ZENICA STEEL WORKS. THE EARLY IRON FOUNDERS WOULD CERTAINLY BE AMAZED AT THE SIGHT OF THE FIERY STREAMS POURING OUT OF THE FURNACES OF YUGOSLAVIA'S LARGEST STEEL WORKS. STEEL OUTPUT INCREASED FROM A PRE-WAR ANNUAL TOTAL OF ABOUT 23,000 TONS TO 1,700,000 TONS IN 1964.

HOW MANY TRADESMEN WERE NEEDED TO PRODUCE AS MUCH FIRE-CLAY AS IS MANUFACTURED IN THE FIRE-CLAY FACTORY AT MLADENOVAC.

MAN INVENTED THE LATHE SO AS TO SHAPE WITH ITS SHARP EDGES, AMONG OTHER THINGS, THIS GIGANTIC AXLE IN THE »RADE KONČAR« ELECTRIC EQUIPMENT FACTORY IN ZAGREB. IN ADDITION TO TEN DEPARTMENTS, THERE IS AN ELECTROTECHNICAL INSTITUTE WITH A HIGH-TENSION LABORATORY IN THE FACTORY, AN INSTITUTE FOR DYNAMIC TESTING OF CURRENTS UP TO 150,000 AMPÈRES, AN INSTITUTE FOR AUTOMATION AND REGULATION, ETC.

WITH HOW LITTLE MATERIAL THIS SLIM AND ELEGANT, BUT YET STURDY ROOF STRUCTURE OF A NEW HALL IN THE NITROGEN WORKS IN PANČEVO IS BEING ERECTED. ITS PRODUCTS WILL MAKE FERTILE LAND EVEN MORE FERTILE.

IN SPITE OF ALL TECHNICAL DEVELOPMENT MAN HAS PRESERVED HIS ORIGINAL DESIRE FOR THE MONUMENTAL AND THE BEAUTIFUL WHICH IS MANIFESTED IN THIS WONDERFUL DOME OF THE BELGRADE FAIR, ONE OF THE LARGEST DOMES IN THE WORLD, CARRIED OUT BY MEANS OF A SPECIAL CONCRETE STRUCTURE.

IN SPITE OF ALL TECHNICAL DEVELOPMENT MAN HAS PRESERVED HIS ORIGINAL DESIRE FOR THE MONUMENTAL AND THE BEAUTIFUL WHICH IS MANIFESTED IN THIS WONDERFUL DOME OF THE BELGRADE FAIR, ONE OF THE LARGEST DOMES IN THE WORLD, CARRIED

MANUFACTURING A TURBINE AT THE »LITOSTROJ« WORKS IN LJUBLJANA, ONE OF THE LARGEST YUGOSLAV FACTORIES ERECTED AFTER THE WAR.

MAN HAS KNOWN SOAP FOR COUNTLESS YEARS, BUT IMPROVED ITS PRODUCTION VERY SLOWLY UNTIL AUTOMATION WAS CARRIED OUT, AS FOR EXAMPLE IN »SAPONIJA«, OSIJEK, THE MOST IMPORTANT YUGOSLAV FACTORY OF SOAP, DETERGENTS, AND COSMETICS.

TWO VIEWS OF THE GIGANTIC »RADE KONČAR« WORKS IN ZAGREB, ONE OF THE MOST OUTSTANDING MANUFACTURERS OF ELECTRICAL EQUIPMENT IN EUROPE.

THE YUGOSLAV WORKER BUILT HIS INDUSTRY, HE WORKS IN IT AND GOVERNS IT. THE WORKERS' COUNCIL AT THE TREPČA MINE.

THE MINING AND FOUNDRY BASIN OF BOR. THE COPPER, SILVER, GOLD, LEAD, AND MERCURY DEPOSITS IN YUGOSLAVIA ARE AMONG THE RICHEST IN EUROPE.

ON THE RIGHT: THIS HAPPY SMILE AND GLITTERING PUPIL SEEM TO BE JOYOUSLY SAYING: »I HAVE DEFEATED THEE, EARTH, AND NOW I'M TAKING THE RICHES YOU WERE HIDING DEEP IN YOUR ENTRAILS«.

THE TINY ANT HAS CLIMBED TO THE TOP OF ONE OF THE NUMEROUS HILLS WHICH HE DUG UP WITH GREAT PERSEVERANCE ALL ROUND THE LARGE VELENJE COAL MINE. IN 1939 YUGOSLAVIA PRODUCED 7 MILLION TONS OF COAL AND IN 1964 29.5 MILLION TONS.

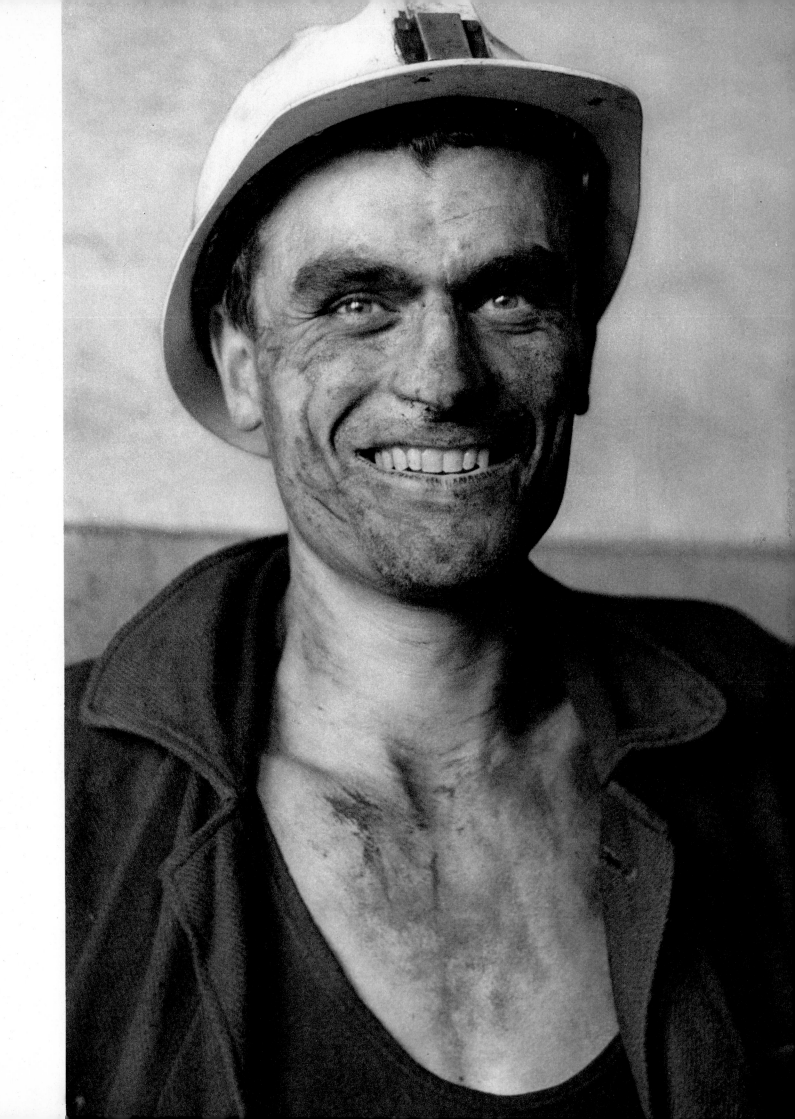

DETAIL FROM A NEW PAPER MILL IN ZAGREB. WHO KNOWS HOW CIVILISATION AND CULTURE WOULD HAVE DEVELOPED IF, SAY, ANCIENT MAN HAD SUCCEEDED IN PRODUCING AS MUCH PAPER AS IS TODAY MANUFACTURED BY AN AVERAGE FACTORY.

OKI (ORGANIC CHEMICAL WORKS IN ZAGREB), THE LARGEST COMBINE OF THIS KIND IN THE COUNTRY. THE COMBINE PRODUCES PLASTICS AND ORGANIC CHEMICALS (60,000 TONS OF POLYETYLENE, POLYSTYRENE, PHENOL, STYRENE, ACETONE, AND VARIOUS CHEMICAL BY-PRODUCTS.) OKI SUPPLIES A NUMBER OF CHEMICAL WORKS WITH RAW MATERIALS, PLASTICS FOR THE BUILDING INDUSTRY, AGRICULTURE AND IT ALSO MANUFACTURES CONSUMER GOODS.

DETAILS FROM THE ORGANIC CHEMICAL WORKS IN ZAGREB (ABOVE) AND THE JUGOVINIL PLASTICS FACTORY NEAR SPLIT (RIGHT).
IN THE DENSE WOOD OF TREES WITHOUT BRANCHES, BOTH THE MAN AND WOMAN SEEM TO BE VERY MUCH AT HOME.

IN SPITE OF THE FACT THAT THE WOMAN WAS PRACTICALLY ENSLAVED FOR CENTURIES, ATTACHED TO THE HOUSE AND ITS CHORES, SHE HAS QUICKLY GOT USED TO VARIOUS JOBS THAT SEEMED TO BE MEANT FOR MEN ONLY. WITH EQUAL SKILL AS MAN SHE SOLDERS METAL AT THE »OBOD« FACTORY IN CETINJE (ABOVE) OR PLACES SHOES ON BOOT-TREES IN THE FOOTWEAR FACTORY IN SKOPJE (RIGHT).

ON THE LEFT: THE »BORIS KIDRIČ« NUCLEAR INSTITUTE AT VINČA NEAR BELGRADE, THE LARGEST SCIENTIFIC INSTITUTE OF THIS KIND IN THE COUNTRY. RESEARCH IN REACTOR PHYSICS IS ONE OF THE BASIC ACTIVITIES OF THE INSTITUTE IN THE FIELD OF NUCLEAR REACTORS. THE INSTITUTE ALSO PRODUCES COBALT BOMBS, ORGANISES SUMMER SCHOOLS FOR NUCLEAR PHYSICS, WHERE THE LECTURERS AND LISTENERS INCLUDE SOME OF THE BEST-KNOWN YUGOSLAV AND FOREIGN SCIENTISTS. MEMBERS OF THE INSTITUTE HAVE SUBMITTED TEN PIECES OF WORK TO THE THIRD GENEVA CONFERENCE FOR THE PEACEFUL USE OF NUCLEAR ENERGY.

IN SOCIALIST YUGOSLAVIA WORKERS RUN ALL FACTORIES AND FIRMS THROUGH THEIR WORKERS' COUNCILS WHICH ARE ELECTED EACH YEAR. IN THESE COUNCILS THERE ARE OVER HALF A MILLION WORKING PEOPLE OF YUGOSLAVIA.

AFTER HE HAS SET INTO OPERATION THE LARGEST WATER POWER PLANT IN YUGOSLAVIA (HE »SPLIT«, NEAR OMIŠ) IN FRONT OF A HUGE MASS OF PEOPLE PRESIDENT TITO ADDRESSED THE PEOPLE AT A MASS MEETING WHERE HE DEALT WITH THE IMPORTANT ACHIEVEMENTS OF THE WORKING PEOPLE OF YUGOSLAVIA. AMONG OTHER THINGS THE PRESIDENT SAID: "YUGOSLAVIA APPROACHED INDUSTRIALISATION, AND NOT ONLY INDUSTRIALISATION, BUT THE WHOLE PROCESS OF HER RECOVERY, RESURRECTED, AND TODAY SHE IS NOT ANY WHAT SHE USED TO BE".

SPEAKING AT THE SAME MEETING, PRESIDENT TITO SAID WHILE DEALING WITH THE ROLE OF THE WORKING MAN IN OUR SOCIETY: "AND THEN: THE WORKERS' SELF-GOVERNMENT HAS HELPED OUR COUNTRY TO MAKE GREAT STRIDES FORWARD, IT HAS CONTRIBUTED TO THE FACT THAT OUR WORKING MAN HAS REALISED ITS CREATIVE ABILITY AND ENERGY. THIS WAS THE FOUNDATION STONE WICH ENABLED US TO BUILD ON SO RAPIDLY".

FROM THE EIGHTH CONGRESS OF THE UNION OF COMMUNISTS OF YUGOSLAVIA, HELD BETWEEN THE 7th AND 13th DECEMBER 1964 IN BELGRADE. IN ADDITION TO 1442 YUGOSLAV DELEGATS THE CONGRESS WAS ATTENDED BY 30 DELEGATIONS OF COMUNIST, SOCIALIST AND OTHER PARTIES FROM 27 COUNTRIES IN EUROPE, ASIA, AFRICA AND LATIN AMERICA. OVER 200 DELEGATES TOOK PART IN THE DISCUSSION, APPROACHING VARIOUS SOCIAL, POLITICAL AND ECONOMIC PROBLEMS OF OUR TIMES WITH THOROUGH-NESS AND SERIOUSNESS. IN HIS CONCLUDING WORDS THE SECRETARY GENERAL OF THE UNION OF COMMUNISTS IN YUGOSLAVIA APPEALED TO THE DELEGATES AND THE WHOLE POPULATION TO HELP THE REALISATION OF THE RESOLUTIONS ADOPTED AT THE EIGHT CONGRESS WHICH MUST BECOME THE GOAL OF THE ACTIVITIES OF THE WORKING PEOPLE OF YUGOSLAVIA.

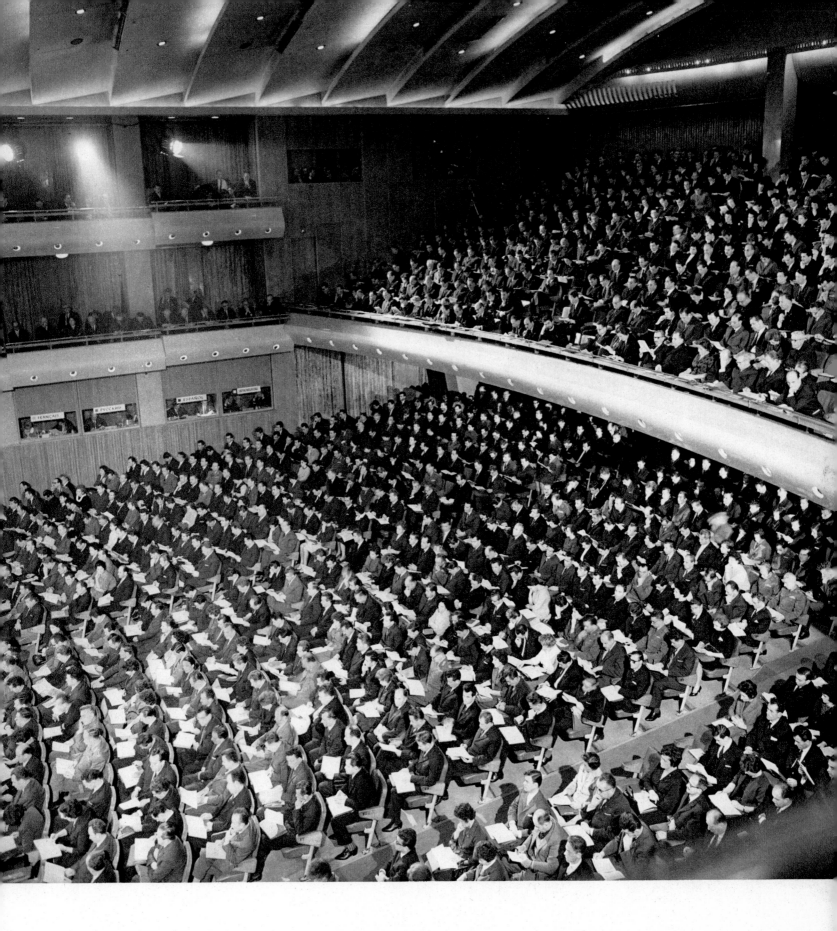

STARTING FROM THE NEED OF FURTHER DEVELOPMENT OF SOCIALIST RELATIONS BASED ON THE PRINCIPLES OF SOCIAL SELF-GOVERN-MENT AND THE DISTRIBUTION OF INCOME IN ACCORDANCE WITH THE EFFECT OF WORK, THE GROWTH OF THE MEANS OF PRODUC-TION IN THE COUNTRY, THE STRENGHENING OF THE POSITION OF THE WORKING MAN IN ALL FIELDS WHERE DECISIONS ARE MADE ON SOCIAL MATTERS, THE CONSOLIDATION OF EQUALITY, BROTHERHOOD AND UNITY OF THE PEOPLES OF YUGOSLAVIA, DEMOCRATIC AND FRIENDLY RELATIONS BETWEEN NATIONS AND STATES, THE INDEPENDENT AND FREE INTERNAL DEVELOPMENT OF ALL PEOPLES, THE PRESERVATION OF PEACE AND PROGRESS OF SOCIALISM IN THE WORLD TODAY — THE EIGHTH CONGRESS HASS SUPPLIED A WIDE ANALYSIS OF RESULTS AND SUCCESSES, WEAKNESSES AND DIFFICULTIES, WHILE AT THE SAME TIME PRODUCING CLEAR DIRECTIVES FOR THE FURTHER STRUGGLE OF COMMUNISTS AND OTHER WORKING PEOPLE.

PHYSICALLY AND MENTALLY HEALTHY NEW GENERATIONS ARE THE BASIC CONDITIONS FOR THE FUTURE OF EACH PEOPLE AND MANKIND
AS A WHOLE. THAT IS WHY SO MUCH CARE IS DEVOTED TO THE UPBRINGING OF CHILDREN, TO THE DEVELOPMENT OF THEIR PHYSI-
CAL AND MENTAL ABILITIES.

THE MOTHER AND CHILD UNICEF CENTRE IN ZAGREB, ONE OF THE MOST MODERN ESTABLISHMENTS OF THIS KIND, WHERE YOUNG MOTHERS ARE INSTRUCTED ON THE LATEST DEVELOPMENTS IN CHILD-CARE AND EDUCATION.

FAIRS — THIS ANCIENT FORM OF TRADE — HAVE NOT BEEN LIMITED TO THE DISPLAY AND EXCHANGE OF GOODS IN PRE-HISTORIC TIMES AND LATER, BUT HAVE ALSO PLAYED AN IMPORTANT SOCIAL AND CULTURAL ROLE. IN ADDITION TO TRADING MAN ALSO DISCUSSED HIS EXPERIENCE, EXCHANGED THOUGHTS AND OPINIONS, HIS KNOWLEDGE AND HIS ARTEFACTS. FAIRS HAVE BEEN HELD IN ZAGREB SINCE THE 11th CENTURY. VIEW OF PART OF THE NEW ZAGREB FAIR (ABOVE AND RIGHT), WHICH IS IN ITS SPACE, THE AMOUNT OF GOODS ON DISPLAY, AND THE NUMBER OF EXHIBITORS (FROM ALL CONTINENTS) ONE OF THE LARGEST FAIRS IN THE WORLD. OVER TWO MILLION VISITORS VISIT THE ZAGREB SPRING AND AUTUMN FAIRS.

KINDERGARTEN IN THE MINING VILLAGE OF VELENJE. MODERN MAN HAS ORGANISED KINDERGARTENS AND NURSERY SCHOOL WHERE CHILDREN OF PRE-SCHOOL AGE CAN STAY WHILE THEIR PARENTS ARE AT WORK. BUT THESE KINDERGARTENS ARE NOT ONLY WAITING ROOMS FOR PARENTS, BUT ALSO THE FIRST SCHOOL: HERE CHILDREN DEVELOP AS SOCIAL BEINGS AND LEARN HOW TO PLAY WITH OTHER CHILDREN, HERE THEY MAKE THEIR FIRST STEPS IN DRAWING, MUSIC, DANCE AND LITERATURE,

SINCE ANCIENT TIMES MAN HAS PROCLAIMED SOME DAYS IN THE YEAR HIS HOLIDAYS AND CELEBRATED THEM IN A SPECIAL WAY...
THE NEW YEAR IS THE COMMON HOLIDAY OF THE WHOLE MANKIND... AND HERE WE CAN SEE PRESIDENT TITO CELEBRATING ONE
OF THE JOYFUL NEW YEARS IN ZAGREB.

IN THIS HUGE HALL OF THE BELGRADE FAIR BOXING MATCHES OFTEN TAKE PLACE, THRILLING THOUSANDS OF PASSIONATE SPECTATORS.

CLOTHING IS NOT USED BY MAN ONLY AS PROTECTION AGAINST THE COLD, BUT ALSO AS EMBELLISHMENT, AS THE OBVIOUS SIGN OF HIS TASTE AND CULTURE. THIS CAN ALSO BE SEEN AT THE FASHION SHOW IN THIS CROWDED HALL OF THE BELGRADE FAIR.

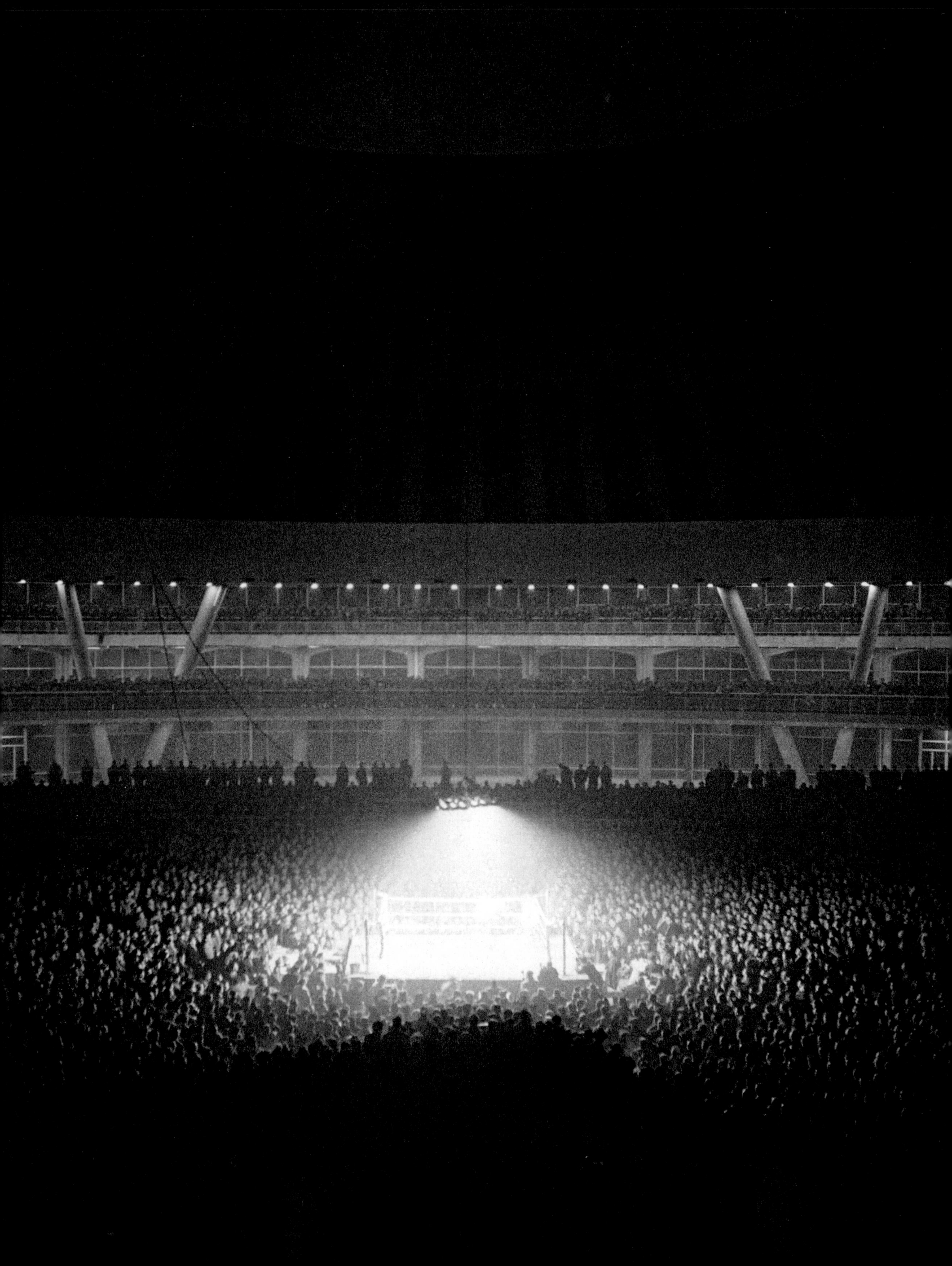

MUSIC WAS THE FIRST ART MAN INVENTED AND PROBABLY IT WILL BE THE LAST ONE HE WILL ABANDON . . . . IN THE HIGHLY ACOUSTIC ATRIUM OF THE RECTOR'S PALACE IN DUBROVNIK, WITHIN THE WELL-KNOWN DUBROVNIK SUMMER FESTIVAL, THE ZAGREB SOLOISTS ARE PLAYING AT ONE OF THEIR NUMEROUS CONCERTS.

FROM THE GALLERY OF THE RECTOR'S PALACE IN DUBROVNIK WOMEN — WHO ALWAYS HAD AN EXCELLENT EAR AND A HEART OPEN TO MUSIC — ARE OBVIOUSLY THRILLED BY THE SOUNDS OF THE VIOLIN.

ON THE RIGHT: THE NAKED WALLS OF THE MEDIEVAL FORTRESS OF LOVRIJENAC IN DUBROVNIK DO NOT LESSEN BUT ON THE CONTRARY INTENSIFY THE POETIC VISION OF THE IMMORTAL ENGLISH PLAYWRIGHT.

BOXES IN THE CROATIAN NATIONAL THEATRE IN ZAGREB .... MAN HAS ALWAYS LIKED BEAUTIFUL WORDS SPOKEN BY ACTORS, HE WAS ALWAYS FOND OF ACTING; IN IT HE RECOGNISED PART OF HIS OWN FEELINGS, DREAMS AND FANTASIES WHICH HE WAS UNABLE TO EXPRESS.

MAN'S TENDENCY FOR VISUAL CLARITY AND THE FREEDOM OF MOVEMENT IN SPACE ARE MANIFESTED IN THIS BOOKSHOP IN ZAGREB, TOO.

MAN'S DESIRE FOR PLAY AND CONTESTS IS MOST CLEARLY MANIFESTED IN CHILDREN WHO ARE NOT HAMPERED BY ANY CONSIDERATIONS THAT GOVERN THE BEHAVIOUR OF GROWN-UPS. THE SQUARES AND STREETS IN BELGRADE ARE LIKE HUGE CANVASES WHERE CHILDREN EXPRESS THEIR DESIRES FOR VISUAL CREATION. THEIR EXCITEMENT IS NOT LESSENED BY THE FACT THAT THE NEXT DAY IMPASSIVE STREET CLEANERS WILL WASH THEIR ACHIEVEMENTS AWAY.

ONE OF THE NUMEROUS HALLS WHERE FUTURE DOCTORS ARE TRAINED. THERE IS NO SUCH FAITHLESS TIME WHEN MAN WOULD NOT ASK FOR MEDICAL HELP WITH CHILDISH FAITH.... AFTER THE UNITED STATES AND THE SOVIET UNION YUGOSLAVIA IS THE FIRST COUNTRY AS TO THE NUMBER OF STUDENTS. IN 1939 THERE WERE 17,000 STUDENT IN YUGOSLAV UNIVERSITIES AND TODAY THIS FIGURE HAS RISEN TO 160,000.

THE LIBRARY AND READING ROOM OF THE »MOŠA PIJADE« WORKERS' UNIVERSITY IN ZAGREB. WORKERS' UNIVERSITIES ARE FOUNDED
IN ALL LARGER INDUSTRIAL CENTRES FOR THE WORKERS' AND EMPLOYEES TO GET ADDITIONAL TRAINING AND QUALIFICATIONS,
TOGETHER WITH GENERAL EDUCATION.

THE BRČKO-BANOVIĆI YOUTH RAILWAY, ERECTED BY THE YOUNG PEOPLE OF YUGOSLAVIA. THE ENERGY OF YOUTH, WASTED IN VARIOUS PARTS OF THE COUNTRY, ON STONE FIELDS AND MOUNTAIN PASTURES, WAS DIRECTED HERE IN ONE HUGE COMMON EFFORT. FOR A GREAT DEAL OF THE YOUTH COMING FROM VILLAGES THE YOUTH RAILWAY AND SIMILAR ACTIONS WERE IDEAL OCCASIONS FOR CULTURAL AND PROFESSIONAL EDUCATION, AND APPROACH TO NEW LIFE.

25 YEARS AGO THE GERMANS KILLED 7,500 CITIZENS OF KRAGUJEVAC ON THESE MEADOWS. MOST OF THEM WERE SECONDARY SCHOOL PUPILS. BUT SUFFERING AND HARDSHIPS SEEM TO HAVE GIVEN UNFORESEEN ENERGY AND VITALITY TO THE PEOPLE. ON THE GRAVES AND PLACES OF DESTRUCTION NEW AND STRONG GENERATIONS ARE GROWING.

LOBBY (ABOVE) AND THE MAIN FRONT (ON THE RIGHT) OF THE »MOŠA PIJADE« WORKERS' UNIVERSITY IN ZAGREB. MODERN ARCHITECTURE, RICH IN SPACE, LIGHT AND AIR, WITHOUT ANY INSIPID ORNAMENTS, FUNCTIONAL AND RATIONAL, MIRRORS THE VIEW OF LIFE OF THE MODERN INDUSTRIALISED TOWN CITIZEN.

EMPIRICISM AND NOT SPECULATION ARE THE MAIN FEATURES OF MODERN MAN. WITHOUT VERIFIED EXPERIMENTS HE WILL NOT TRY TO MATERIALISE HIS OWN PROJECTS. IN THE INSTITUTE FOR SHIP HYDRODYNAMICS IN ZAGREB, CONSISTING OF FOUR BASINS FOR THE TESTING OF SHIP MODELS, TWO CAVITATION TUNNELS AND AN ELECTRONICS LABORATORY, SHIP MODELS ARE TESTED WHICH WILL BE BUILT ONLY AFTER THEY HAVE ACHIEVED THE BEST POSSIBLE RESULTS.

DETAIL FROM THE »BORIS KIDRIČ« ATOMIC INSTITUTE AT VINČA NEAR BELGRADE. THE RESEARCH NUCLEAR REACTOR RA IS ONE OF THE LARGEST OF ITS KIND IN EUROPE. THE INSTITUTE IS DIRECTING ITS ACTIVITIES TO RESEARCH IN ELECTRIC POWER, AND THE BUILD-ING OF A NUCLEAR POWER PLANT HAS BEEN TAKEN INTO CONSIDERATION.

RAFTS NEAR BROD ON THE KUPA. MAN IS FOND OF DEFYING DANGERS. THE FOAMY WHIRLPOOLS OF NUMEROUS RIVERS ARE IRRE-SISTIBLY ALLURING CANOEISTS.

SPORT AND RECREATION HAVE BECOME INDISPENSABLE FOR THE MODERN MAN. AS LATE AS THE 19th CENTURY MOST SAILORS DID NOT KNOW HOW TO SWIM AND TODAY MILLIONS OF BATHERS COME TO THE ADRIATIC COAST, TO THE NUMEROUS RIVERS AND THE INTERIOR OF THE COUNTRY. IN THE INTERIOR MAN BUILDS LARGE SWIMMING POOLS SUCH AS THIS ONE ON TAŠMAJDAN IN BELGRADE.

MAN'S DESIRE FOR
SPORTS AND DANGER-
OUS GAMES MAKES
HIM FIGHT HIS WAY
THROUGH BLIZZARDS
TO REACH THE WON-
DERFUL SKI GROUNDS
ON THE ROMANTIC
ŠAR MOUNTAIN (ON
THE LEFT AND RIGHT)

KUPARI NEAR DUBROVNIK. NEVER IN THE PAST HAS MAN FELT SUCH A KEEN DESIRE FOR THE SEA AND ITS SUNNY BEACHES. BUT THIS DESIRE GOES HAND IN HAND WITH THE DEMAND FOR MODERN HOTELS AND OTHER AMENITIES. WITHIN THE LAST THREE YEARS A NUMBER OF HOTELS HAVE BEEN BUILT WITH A TOTAL OF 35,000 BEDS.

THE PLEASANT CUSTOMS OF THE WARM LITTORAL HAVE BEEN TAKEN OVER IN THE INTERIOR: OPEN-AIR RESTAURANTS AND CAFÉS
ARE POPULAR IN ALL PARTS OF THE COUNTRY. THE SPACIOUS TERRACE OF THE CITY CAFÉ IN BELGRADE WHICH, IN ADDITION TO
COMFORT, IS ATTRACTIVE TO LOOK AT.

SQUARE OF REPUBLIC IN ZAGREB. MAN HAS REPLACED THE MOONLIGHT BY ELECTRIC LIGHTING, BUT THE NIGHT HAS RETAINED ALL ITS MYSTERY.

WHEN LOVE WAKES UP IN THE UNROMANTIC MAN OF OUR TIMES NO TECHNICAL WONDER CAN REPLACE THE BLOSSOMING MEADOW
AT VRNJAČKA BANJA.

AUTUMN IS THE MOST BEAUTIFUL SEASON IN BELGRADE. SOFT, WARM, SUNNY, WITH THE NOSTALGY OF FALLEN LEAVES AND A NOS-
TALGIC LOOK OVER THE WIDE PLACE WHERE THE SAVA AND THE DANUBE MEET, AND FARTHER AWAY OVER THE IMMEASURABLE
PLAIN OF VOJVODINA.

THE INTIMATE WOOD-COVERED WALK ON OLD GRIČ ADDS SPECIAL CHARM TO AUTUMNS IN ZAGREB.

MAN HAS INVENTED FAST AND CHEAP VEHICLES THUS ENABLING CHILDREN VERY EARLY TO GET ACQUAINTED WITH PARTS OF THE COUNTRY AND TOWNS OF WHICH THEIR GRANDPARENTS HARDLY KNEW. THIS GROUP OF CHILDREN IS ONLY ONE OF THE NUMEROUS EXCURSIONS OF PUPILS TRAVELLING THROUGH YUGOSLAVIA.

RAILWAYS AND CARS HAVE BECOME TOO SLOW, AND AIR TRAFFIC IS A NECESSITY OF THE MODERN MAN. HUGE PASSENGER PLANES, AIR-PORTS AND ANCILLARY FACILITIES ARE BUILT... VIEW OF THE LOBBY OF THE LARGEST AIR-PORT IN THE COUNTRY (SURČIN NEAR BELGRADE).

THE ITALIAN PROVERB TO THE EFFECT THAT THE WHOLE WORLD IS ONE PLACE WAS NEVER MORE TRUTHFUL THAN IT IS TODAY. EVEN IN THE SMALL TOWN OF KORČULA — WITH ONLY SOME 2,500 INHABITANTS — WE SHALL COME ACROSS PEOPLE FROM ALL PARTS OF EUROPE AND OTHER CONTINENTS.

A GREAT NUMBER OF FOREIGN AIR COMPANIES HAS INCLUDED YUGOSLAV RESORTS IN THEIR SERVICES. PEOPLE FROM ALL PARTS OF THE WORLD ARRIVE AT THE DUBROVNIK AIR-PORT TO ENJOY THE SEA AND SUNSHINE AND TO ADMIRE THE BEAUTY OF THIS OLD TOWN.

SVETI STEFAN. IT HAS OCCURRED TO MAN THAT HE WILL PRESERVE THE APPEARANCE OF THE OLD FISHING VILLAGE, WHILE TURNING IT INTO A HOTEL. AND HE DID NOT MAKE A MISTAKE: THE PEOPLE OF TODAY, SATED, BUT ON THE OTHER HAND DESIROUS OF ATTRACTIONS, CANNOT EASILY RESIST THE CHARM OF THIS PLACE.

OVER 11 HUNDRED KILOMETRES OF THE ADRIATIC HIGHWAY — CUT INTO ROCKS OR ON IMPRESSIVE BRIDGES — FOLLOW THE
MOST BEAUTIFUL AND MOST INDENTED COAST IN EUROPE, FINALLY REACHING OVER THE MOUNTAINS IN CRNA GORA THE PICTURESQUE
PARTS OF THE INTERIOR AND THE NORTHERN HIGHWAY WICH LINKS THE AUSTRIAN BORDER WITH GREECE.

MODERN, COMFORTABLE ARCHITECTURE DEPRIVES TRADITIONAL TOWNS OF THEIR INDIVIDUAL APPEARANCE AND GIVES THEM THEIR NEW UNIFORM PHYSIOGNOMY. THESE BLOCKS OF FLATS IN ZAGREB (LEFT) COULD BE AS WELL IN SKOPJE (ABOVE), AND THOSE FROM SKOPJE COULD HAVE BEEN BUILT IN ZAGREB, AND NOTHING WOULD HAVE CHANGED THE APPEARANCE AND THE SPIRIT OF THESE TOWNS.

QUICK INDUSTRIALISATION LEADS TO RAPID INCREASE OF THE TOWN POPULATION THE PEASANT POPULATION IN YUGOSLAVIA SHRANK FROM 75 PER CENT TO 50 PER CENT IN POST WAR YEARS. THIS HAS LED TO INCREASED BUILDING ACTIVITIES IN RECENT YEARS. BOTH ZAGREB (ABOVE) AND BELGRADE (BELOW) ARE PREPARING BUILDING SITES ON PRE-WAR TOWN TERRITORY, AND AT THE SAME TIME NEW HOUSING ESTATES ARE UNDER CONSTRUCTION IN ZAGREB ON THE RIGHT BANK, AND IN BELGRADE ON THE LEFT BANK OF THE SAVA, FOR NEW PARTS OF THE TOWN THAT WILL INCLUDE A QUARTER OF A MILLION INHABITANTS IN EITHER TOWN. IN 1952 35,000 FLATS, WERE BUILT AND SINCE THEN THE BUILDING OF BLOCKS OF FLATS WERE BUILT AND SHORTLY THIS FIGURE WILL REACH 200,000 A YEAR.

HOTEL IN TITOGRAD. THE ERECTION OF LARGE COMFORTABLE HOTELS IN RESORTS AND LARGER CENTRES IS ONE OF THE ESSENTIAL FEATURES OF THE PRESENT BUILDING ACTIVITIES.

HOTEL AT PRIŠTINA, THE CAPITAL OF KOSOVO AND METOHIJA. THE EVER INCREASING MOVEMENTS OF TOURISTS AND BUSINESS PEOPLE REQUIRES THE ERECTION OF NEW HOTELS IN ALL TOWN OF THE COUNTRY.

NEW BELGRADE. ON THE SANDY AND SWAMPY GROUNDS NEAR THE PLACE WHERE THE SAVA FLOWS INTO THE DANUBE A MODERN SETTLEMENT IS GROWING, EQUIPPED WITS FACILITIES AND AMENITIES FOR 250,000 INHABITANTS.

NEW YEAR CELEBRATION IN THE HUGE HALL OF BELGRADE FAIR. THE PRATER FROM VIENNA STILL FINDS AN AN ECHO IN MANY EUROPEAN TOWNS.

PLANICA — ONE OF THE LARGEST AND BEST-KNOWN SKI JUMPS IN THE WORLD. THE FIRST JUMP OVER 100 METRES WAS ACHIEVED HERE.

ANOTHER VIEW OF PLANICA WHICH ATTRACTS HUNDREDS OF SKIERS AND THOUSANDS OF ENTHUSIASTIC SPECTATORS EVERY YEAR.

THE DESIRE FOR MOVEMENT, FOR ENERGETIC ACTIVITIES AND CHANGE ATTRACTS THOUSANDS OF SKIERS TO THE SNOW-COVERED SLOPES WHERE THEY EXPOSE THEIR SKIN TO THE WARM SUNSHINE OF THE MOUNTAINS — THE SKIN WILL SOON BE TANNED ON THE MAGIC HEIGHTS OF JAHORINA.

THE KAMNIŠKE ALPS. THERE IS SOMETHING MORE THAN THE NEED OF RECREATION THAT MAKES MODERN MAN CLIMB STEEP MOUN-
TAINS AND CONQUER DANGEROUS MOUNTAIN PEAKS.

FOOTBALL STADIUM IN ZAGREB. HOWEVER HIGH MAN HAS RISEN WITH THE HELP OF MODERN TECHNICAL MEANS, EVEN IF REACHING PLANETS WITH THE UTMOST EASE OF TAKING A WALK, EVEN IF HAS CHANGED HIS SURROUNDINGS, ONE THING MAN CANNOT CHANGE: HUMAN NATURE. BREAD AND GAMES SINCE ROMAN TIMES UP TO OUR OWN DAYS.

WITH THE SAME ENTHUSIAM OUR GREATFATHERS WATCHED THE MAGNIFICENT FLIGHT OF BIRDS AS WE ARE WATCHING OUR COM-
RADES TODAY — ICARUS' OLD DREAM HAS BECOME ONLY A TOO PEDESTRIAN REALITY.

OF THE GYMNASTIC GATHERINGS THE MOST INTERESTING IS THE "PARADE OF YOUTH" HELD EACH YEAR ON THE STADIUM OF THE YUGOSLAV PEOPLE'S ARMY IN BELGRADE.

HOW MANY CENTURIES LIE BETWEEN ILLYRIAN GRAVES, ROMAN SARCOPHAGI, MEDIEVAL BOGUMIL TOMBSTONES AND MODERN STEEL, CONCRETE AND ASPHALT! THE SAME CENTURIES STILL SEPARATE THE PRIMITIVE MAN, IN HIS HOVELS IN INACCESSIBLE MOUNTAINS FROM THE INDUSTRIALISED MAN WHO CANNOT BE SURPRISED BY ANY NEW TECHNICAL WONDER. AND YET, UNDER THE EXTERNAL SPLENDOUR OF CIVILISATION AND UNDER THE EXTERNAL POVERTY AND BACKWARDNESS THE SAME MAN IS LIVING — WITH THE SAME BLOOD AND PASSIONS, COURAGE AND FEARS, LOVE AND HATRED ... WITH THE SAME CHILDISH JOYS AND LAUGHTER.

AUTHORS — SELECTION AND COMPILATION: ZDUNIĆ DRAGUTIN ● ARTWORK: KINERT ALBERT ● TEXT BY: KAPIČIĆ JOVO, OREL TINE, RAOŠ IVAN, TOMAŠEVIĆ NEBOJŠA ● VERSES BY — JAKŠIĆ ĐURA: FATHERLAND; JENKO SIMON: TO THE MOUNTAIN; KAŠTELAN JURE: A FORTRESS THAT DOES NOT SURRENDER; KONESKI BLAŽE: »TEŠKOTO«; MILIČEVIĆ NIKOLA: THE OLD COUNTRY; PETAR PETROVIĆ NJEGOŠ: VERSES FROM »GORSKI VIJENAC« (THE MOUNTAIN WREATH); ŠANTIĆ ALEKSA: SPRING ● PHOTOGRAPHS BY: BABIĆ MILAN, ČAĆE NEDELJKO, DABAC TOŠO, DEBELJKOVIĆ BRANIMIR, DRNKOV BLAGOJE, GRČEVIĆ MLADEN, HRELJANOVIĆ VIKTOR, JOVANOVIĆ BLAGOJE, KARAMATIJEVIĆ PAVLE, KRČADI-NAC ŽELJKO, MARCUTTI NINO, MINČEV ALEKSANDAR, PAVIĆ MILAN, PAVLOVIĆ MILOŠ, RENDULIĆ DRAGO, SZABO MARIJAN, ŠURJAK ZLATKO, TURIN BRANKO, ZUBER VILKO

COLLABORATORS — EDITOR IN CHIEF: ZDUNIĆ DRAGUTIN ● READER: MILEUSNIĆ OZREN ● PROOF-READER: UZORINAC ZDENKO ● TRANS-LATOR OF VERSES: BEKER MIROSLAV ● TRANSLATOR OF PROSE: ČIČIN ŠAIN ANTE, BEKER MIROSLAV ● PUBLISHER: PUBLISHING SECTION OF GRAPHIC INSTITUTION OF CROATIA, 2, PRILAZ JNA, ZAGREB ● FOR THE PUBLISHERS: HRBUD JOSIP — MANAGER OF GRAPHIC INSTITUTION OF CROATIA, LEŠIĆ VID — MANAGER OF THE PUBLISHING SECTION ● PRINTED BY: GRAPHIC INSTITUTION OF CROATIA, 26, FRANKOPANSKA, ZAGREB ● PRINTED IN 1967 IN 15.000 COPIES ● ISSUED IN: SERBIAN-CROATIAN, FRENCH, ENGLISH, GERMAN ● TISAK: GRAFIČKI ZAVOD HRVATSKE, ZAGREB, FRANKOPANSKA 26, JUGOSLAVIJA, 1967.